PHP

MIKE McGRATH

BARNES
&NOBLE
BOOKS
NEW YORK

In easy steps is an imprint of Computer Step
Southfield Road . Southam
Warwickshire CV47 0FB . United Kingdom
www.ineasysteps.com

This edition published for Barnes & Noble Books, New York
FOR SALE IN THE USA ONLY
www.bn.com

Notice of Liability
Every effort has been made to ensure that this book contains
accurate and current information. However, Computer Step and the
author shall not be liable for any loss or damage suffered by readers
as a result of any information contained herein.

Trademarks
All trademarks are acknowledged as belonging to their respective
companies.

Printed and bound in the United Kingdom

ISBN 0-7607-4786-5

Contents

1   Introducing PHP   **7**

PHP in this book	8
What is PHP?	9
How does PHP work?	10
Creating a PHP environment	11
Installing Apache	12
Starting & stopping Apache	13
Installing MySQL	14
Installing PHP	15
Configuring Apache for PHP	16
Testing PHP	17
Testing MySQL connection	18

2   PHP environment in Linux   **19**

Installing MySQL	20
Installing Apache	22
Configuring Apache	24
Running Apache	25
Installing PHP	26
Configuring Apache for PHP	28
Testing PHP	29
Testing MySQL connection	30

3   Getting started with PHP   **31**

Hello world	32
Syntax rules	33
Escaping characters	34
Reserved words	35
Variables	36
Data types	37
Functions	38
Function arguments	39
Multiple functions	40
Variable scope	41
Multiple arguments	42

4   Performing operations   **43**

Arithmetical operators	44
Logical operators	46
Assignment operators	48
Comparison operators	50
Conditional operator	52

Making statements 53

5

Conditional if statement	54
If-else statement	55
Switch statement	56
For loop	57
While loop	58
Do-while loop	59
Interrupting loops	60
Return statement	62

Using arrays 63

6

Creating an array	64
Changing array element values	65
Listing array elements	66
Getting the array size	67
Adding & removing array elements	68
Array keys and values	70
One-base indexing	71
Manipulating arrays	72

Generating dynamic content 73

7

Identifying browser & platform	74
Server date & time	76
Time-specific content	77
Random number generator	78
Getting form values	80
Displaying submitted values	81
Manipulating submitted values	82
String manipulation	84
Reloading a page	86
Browser redirection	88
PHP and mobile devices	90

File handling with PHP 91

8

Displaying directory files	92
Copying & renaming files	94
Deleting files	96
Opening & closing files	97
Reading a file	98
Writing a file	100
Logging visitor details	102
Enabling file uploads	104
Creating an upload form	105
Creating an upload script	106
Uploading a file	107
Confirming file upload	108

9

Data persistence — 109

Introducing cookies	110
Set a cookie	112
Access limitation	114
Introducing sessions	116
Starting a session	118
Sessions without cookies	120
Setting session preferences	122
Cookies or sessions?	124

10

Sending email with PHP — 125

Enabling PHP email	126
Creating a feedback form	127
Sending plain text email	128
Sending HTML email	130
Creating an attachment form	132
Sending attachments with email	134
Adding error-checking	136
Validating email address formats	138

11

Getting started with MySQL — 139

Introducing databases	140
Exploring database tables	141
Creating a new database	142
Creating a database table	143
SQL data types	144
SQL field modifiers	145
Inserting table data	146
Altering an existing table	147
Updating records	148
Deleting data, tables & databases	149
SQL queries	150

12

PHP & MySQL together — 151

Creating a MySQL user & password	152
Connecting a user to MySQL	153
Listing databases	154
Listing table names	155
Creating a database	156
Deleting a database	157
Creating a database table	158
Inserting table data	161
Altering tables	163
Retrieving data from a table	164
More MySQL	166

User authentication   167

13

Creating a user table   168
Adding authorized users   170
Displaying authorized users   172
The user log-in form   174
The log-in form-handler script   175
An authenticated log-in attempt   176

A PHP guestbook   177

14

Creating a guestbook database table   178
Signing the guestbook   180
Inserting guestbook entries   182
Using timestamp data   183
Viewing the guestbook   184
More PHP resources   186

Index   187

Introducing PHP

This chapter introduces **PHP**: **H**ypertext **P**reprocessor (PHP). It defines what PHP is, and how it works, then demonstrates how to establish a working environment for PHP on the Windows operating system.

Covers

PHP in this book | 8

What is PHP? | 9

How does PHP work? | 10

Creating a PHP environment | 11

Installing Apache | 12

Starting & stopping Apache | 13

Installing MySQL | 14

Installing PHP | 15

Configuring Apache for PHP | 16

Testing PHP | 17

Testing MySQL connection | 18

Chapter One

PHP in this book

This book is an introduction to the **P**HP:**H**ypertext **P**reprocessor (PHP) server-side scripting language using examples to demonstrate each step.

PHP can be used to create interactive dynamic websites and is rapidly gaining in popularity because it is a flexible, cross-platform technology that provides amazingly powerful features.

You may have visited some impressive Web sites where the URL address ends with a file extension of **.phtml**, **.php**, **.php3** or **.php4**. These are all dynamic Web pages served up to the Web browser using the power of the PHP scripting language on the server.

The examples given throughout this book detail the source code and the resultant output that appears in the Web browser.

What you need to know

PHP code in interspersed between HTML code in the original PHP document on the server, so it is expected that you are familiar with the **H**yper**T**ext **M**arkup **L**anguage (HTML).

Examples relating to databases use commands from the **S**tructured **Q**uery **L**anguage (SQL). Previous knowledge of SQL is helpful but not essential as this book includes an introduction to basic SQL commands in a chapter introducing MySQL relational databases.

Those readers with some experience of other scripting languages, such as JavaScript, will more quickly understand some of the examples but no previous knowledge of scripting is assumed by the book's text. You do not need to be a JavaScript guru to learn PHP.

Required software

Downloading the latest release of Apache, MySQL and PHP is tedious but does ensure that you are working with the most up-to-date versions.

The book provides instructions to create a PHP development environment under both Windows and Linux operating systems. This requires that you download the latest versions of the free Apache Web server, the free MySQL database server and the free PHP processor itself.

Instructions are provided later in this chapter on how to download, install and test Apache, MySQL and PHP on a Windows platform.

Instructions for similar installation of versions for Unix-based operating systems are given in chapter 2 using the Linux platform.

What is PHP?

PHP originally stood for **P**ersonal **H**ome **P**age and was created in 1994 by an independent I.T. contractor named Rasmus Lerdorf. This was simply a set of Perl scripts he wrote to track visitors to his Web site and to log information about them. Very soon he received enquiries about these scripts from other people so rewrote them as a scripting engine that included a **F**orm **I**nterpreter. The revised package was released in 1996 as **PHP-FI** to reflect its new features.

Developers around the world began contributing ideas and by 1997 over 50,000 Web sites were using **PHP-FI** for a variety of dynamic functions. Two of these developers, Zeev Suraski and Andi Gutmans, were primarily responsible for creating an **A**pplication **P**rogramming **I**nterface (API) that became the PHP parser which was released in June 1998 as **PHP3**.

For more information about PHP and the Zend engine please refer to www.zend.com/aboutphp.php.

The updated version of **PHP4** incorporates the Zend engine so that PHP scripting can be used with any combination of Web server, operating system and platform. PHP is now used in over 7 million domains worldwide and its popularity continues to grow.

The stated goal of PHP is "To allow Web developers to write dynamically generated pages quickly". Its usefulness includes the ability to read & write files, gather & process form data, send data via email, access & manipulate database records, read & write cookies, maintain data in session variables, facilitate user authentication, provide data encryption and much, much more.

Advantages of PHP

In addition to the cross-platform abilities mentioned above, PHP offers **speed** of execution using only meagre system resources so will not slow down the host machine. It uses its own resource management system, and has a sophisticated method for handling variables, thereby ensuring **stability**.

PHP provides many levels of **security** which can be set in its initialization file to the desired level. Its **simplicity** allows anyone with just basic knowledge of HTML to start integrating PHP into their pages straight away.

PHP's modular system of extensions provides **extensibility** that allow it to interface with different libraries, such as encryption, graphics or XML, and adding further extensions is very simple.

How does PHP work?

A typical PHP page will contain a number of PHP elements along with HTML markup elements and other textual content.

When a Web browser requests a PHP page from a Web server that is PHP-enabled the server will call up the PHP parser to process all the PHP elements on that page.

The PHP parser executes the PHP script instructions on the page, generating a HTML document that is then sent to the Web browser as a response to the original request.

The PHP parser may also be asked to retrieve information from a database so the entire process appears like the illustration below:

Code that is executed on the server, like PHP, is called "server-side" code whereas code that is executed by the browser, like JavaScript, is called "client-side" code.

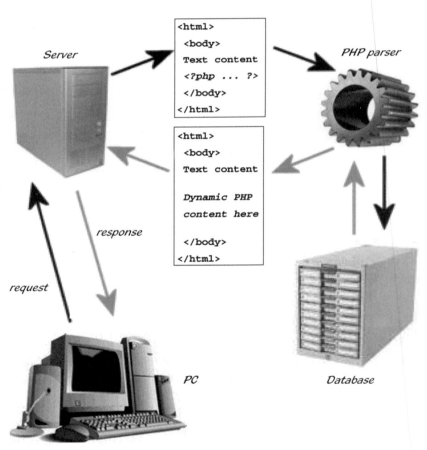

Creating a PHP environment

In order to develop and run PHP Web pages these three vital components need to be installed on the computer system:

Apache

- **Web Server** - PHP will work with virtually all Web server software, including Microsoft's Internet Information Server (IIS), but is most often used with the freely available Apache server. The price and its reliability may explain why Apache is by far the most widely used commercial Web server around the world. All examples in this book have been run on Apache

MySQL

- **Database** - PHP will work with virtually all database software, including Oracle and Sybase, but is most often used with the free MySQL database software for which it has specific optimization. The popularity of MySQL is justified by its speed and scalability which makes it suitable for deployment on high-traffic Web sites. All database examples in this book use MySQL.

- **PHP parser** - In order to process PHP script instructions a parser must be installed to generate HTML output that can be sent to the Web browser. The parser engine is identical irrespective of the operating system so PHP pages need no change to run on different platforms. All examples in this book use the PHP4 parser.

Windows

As the Windows platform is by far the most popular desktop operating system it is convenient to establish a PHP environment in Windows to develop and test PHP Web pages. These pages may then be run live on Windows or be uploaded to a Web server running a different operating system.

The rest of this chapter demonstrates how to download and install each of the three components needed to establish a PHP environment on a Windows platform.

The acronym **LAMP** is sometimes used to describe the most popular PHP environment configuration. The initials refer to Linux, **A**pache, **M**ySQL and **P**HP. Unix-based Web servers are by far the most common worldwide and of these the totally free Linux operating system is the favored platform. Linux provides the reliability needed for minimum downtime and has robust security.

Linux users can skip ahead to chapter two which demonstrates how to establish a PHP environment on a Linux platform.

Installing Apache

Apache is the world's most popular web server which, according to a recent survey, accounts for 56% of all web servers worldwide. It can be freely downloaded from **http://httpd.apache.org** or one of the mirrors listed on that site.

Download the latest stable version for Windows – this will be named something like **apache_1.3.23-win32-x86-no_src.msi**. Double-click on the downloaded file to begin installation then complete the input fields in the **Server Information** dialog box so that it looks like the illustration below:

*Ensure that you name the server **localhost** and that the radio button to **Run Apache as a service for All Users** is selected.*

Install at C:\ to automatically create an Apache directory structure at C:\Apache.

The Apache default page is similar to that shown in the screenshot at the bottom of page 25.

When the **Setup Type** dialog box appears choose the option to have a **complete** installation. Finally, in the **Destination Folder** dialog box enter a convenient location for the Apache directory structure, such as **C:** then complete the installation.

The Apache server will now be running in the background. To verify this open a web browser and type **http://localhost** in the address field then press **enter** to display the default Apache page.

Starting & stopping Apache

If Apache has been installed with the recommended option to **Run as a service for All Users** it will constantly run in the background and so be available via **http://localhost** at any time.

Alternatively if Apache has been installed with the option to **Run when started manually** it can be started from the command line by typing **NET START apache** at a prompt. Similarly it can be stopped by typing **NET STOP apache**. In each case a status comment is reported in the command window, like this:

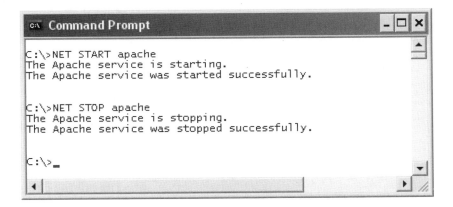

Either of these techniques can also be used to start and stop the MySQL server.

An alternative means of controlling background services is available on modern Windows platforms, like Windows XP. All possible services can be displayed by navigating through **Start > Settings > Control Panel > Administrative Tools > Services**. Click on the **Apache** service in the list then select the option to **Stop** or **Restart** the service. When Apache is stopped an option to **Start the service** is displayed which you can click to start Apache running again.

Installing MySQL

There are a variety of database servers available for purchase, such as Microsoft Access, but the MySQL database server is both powerful and free. It is in widespread use on Web servers running PHP and can be freely downloaded from **http://sourceforge.net/projects/mysql** or **www.mysql.com**.

Download the latest binary release version of MySQL for Windows from the web site, such as **mysql-3.23.49-win.zip**. Unzip this file then double-click on the extracted file called **setup.exe** to start the installation. During setup choose a convenient location for the installation, such as **C:\MySQL**. The installation includes a folder named **Docs** containing helpful guidance in a file called **manual.html**.

Before the MySQL database server can be started the configuration file **C:\MySQL\my-example.cnf** must be copied to the root directory at **C:** and renamed to **my.cnf**. The options set in this file are read by MySQL whenever it is started.

The **C:\MySQL\bin** folder contains all the executable files to run MySQL. On Windows XP, 2000 and NT systems MySQL can be installed as a service that runs in the background but other platforms have to run MySQL manually as an application.

On Windows 9x platforms type "C:\mysqld" to start MySQL and type "C:\mysqladmin -u root shutdown" to stop MySQL.

Type **C:\mysql\bin\mysqld-nt —install** at a command prompt to install MySQL as a service that will automatically run in the background. This can be stopped manually from a prompt with the command **NET STOP mysql** and restarted with the command **NET START mysql**. With MySQL running type **C:\MySQL\bin\mysql** to open the MySQL monitor where databases can be created and manipulated:

*The MySQL monitor can be closed to return to a regular prompt by typing **quit** or **exit** at the **mysql>** prompt.*

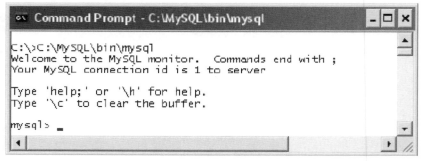

Installing PHP

The final component needed to establish a PHP development environment is the installation of PHP itself. The latest stable release can be freely downloaded from **www.php.net**. This installation example uses version **php-4.1.1-Win32.zip** – the installation procedure may vary for other versions. The contents of this file must be extracted, using any zip file tool like Winzip, to a convenient location, such as **C:\PHP**.

The extracted files include one named **php.ini-dist** that is a template PHP configuration file. Copy this file to your **C:\Windows** folder, where other initialization files are located, then rename the file as **php.ini**.

For more about ***register_globals*** *please refer to the notes on this book's page at:* **www.ineasysteps.com.**

For PHP versions later than 4.1.1. it is essential that you now open **php.ini** in a text editor, like Notepad, and edit the **register_globals** configuration parameter to read **register_globals = On**.

Specifications in the **php.ini** file should have been automatically configured during installation to identify the location of Apache and MySQL, providing they were installed before PHP. For example, under the **Paths and Directories** section the **doc_root** value should be assigned the location **C:\Apache\htdocs** if Apache has been installed at **C:\Apache**, as described on page 12.

To change to the alternative configuration, copy the file ***php.ini-recommended*** *to* **C:\Windows** *and rename it as* ***php.ini.***

By default PHP is installed with a configuration suitable for development purposes and not for on-line production use. There is an alternative PHP configuration template file called **php.ini-recommended** that provides runtime specifications for on-line performance in place of the default configuration. Carefully study the notes in the **php.ini-recommended** file before adopting this as your **php.ini** file and read the important security information available at **http://php.net/manual/en/security.php**.

No installation wizard is needed to install PHP so just extracting the files from the downloaded zip file to **C:\PHP** and setting up the **php.ini** file in **C:\Windows** completes the installation. Before PHP can be tested with a browser, however, modifications need to be made to the Apache configuration so that it can recognize PHP examples and know how to handle them. The ensuing pages in this chapter describe how to modify the Apache configuration and how to test the PHP environment.

Configuring Apache for PHP

Before the Apache server can run PHP examples it must be told how to recognize PHP file types by editing the configuration file **C:\Apache\conf\httpd.conf** to add the PHP MIME types to its list of recognized file types.

MIME is an acronym for Multipurpose Internet Mail Extensions which is a standard for defining file type formats.

Open the **httpd.conf** file in a text editor then find the section relating to the **AddType** instruction. Insert in the **AddType** section these two extra lines to identify the PHP MIME types:

AddType application/x-httpd-php .phtml .php .php3 .php4
AddType application/x-httpd-php-source .phps

Also Apache needs to know the location of the PHP parser in order to handle files with any of the extensions specified along with the PHP MIME types – insert these two lines below the new types:

ScriptAlias /php/ "c:/php/"
Action application/x-httpd-php "/php/php.exe"

The **ScriptAlias** defines the home directory where PHP is installed and the **Action** points to the actual PHP parser file within that directory. So the amended section should now look like this:

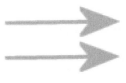

```
#
# AddType allows you to tweak mime.types
# without actually editing it, or to
# make certain files to be certain types.
#
AddType application/x-tar .tgz

AddType application/x-httpd-php .phtml .php .php3 .php4
AddType application/x-httpd-php-source .phps

ScriptAlias /php/ "c:/php/"
Action application/x-httpd-php "/php/php.exe"


#
# AddHandler allows you to map certain file extensions
# to "handlers",actions unrelated to filetype. These can
# be either built into the server or added with the
# Action command
```

Refer back to page 13 for help on starting and stopping Apache.

Save the **httpd.conf** file then restart Apache to apply the changes.

Testing PHP

To create an initial PHP file that can be used to test the environment open a text editor and type this line of code:

```
<?php  phpinfo();  ?>
```

phpinfo.php

Save the file with the name **phpinfo.php** and place it in Apache's **htdocs** folder. This location is where Apache automatically looks for files that have been requested by a web browser.

Now, with Apache running, open a web browser and type into its URL address field **http://localhost/phpinfo.php**. Press **enter** and PHP will generate the web page shown below, listing information about your PHP installation.

Testing MySQL connection

As a final test of the development environment a PHP script can be executed via the Apache web server to ensure that a connection can be made to the MySQL server running on your system. This will effectively involve all three components of the environment.

The test script is listed below within the HTML **body** section of a document. It will be explained in more detail later but, for now, it can be simply copied verbatim to check the MySQL connection. This document has been written in a Windows' Notepad text editor then saved as **mysqltest.php** in Apache's **htdocs** folder.

mysqltest.php

```
<html>
<head> <title>MySQL Connection Test</title> </head>
<body>
<h2>

<?php
  $connection = mysql_connect("localhost","root","")
   or die("Sorry - unable to connect to MySQL");
   echo("Congratulations - you connected to MySQL");
?>

</h2>
</body> </html>
```

When **http://localhost/mysqltest.php** is requested in a browser address field the PHP parser executes the script code and a message will appear in the generated HTML output stating the test result. If the test succeeds the generated output looks like this screenshot:

PHP environment in Linux

This chapter demonstrates how to establish a working environment for PHP on the Linux operating system to include MySQL database software, the Apache web server and the PHP processor itself. The environment setup for Windows was demonstrated in the previous chapter so Windows users can skip ahead to chapter three.

Covers

Installing MySQL | 20

Installing Apache | 22

Configuring Apache | 24

Running Apache | 25

Installing PHP | 26

Configuring Apache for PHP | 28

Testing PHP | 29

Testing MySQL connection | 30

Chapter Two

Installing MySQL

MySQL is the world's most popular free database software and is in constant daily use on thousands of servers around the globe. It can be freely downloaded from **www.mysql.com** or from **http://sourceforge.net/projects/mysql**.

The recommended method of installation is to use the Redhat Package Manager (RPM) that is included with virtually all versions of Linux. There are several Redhat packages available for download from the MySQL Web site – similar to this selection:

- MySQL 3.23.49 Server (i386) (14.1M)

- MySQL 3.23.49 Client programs (5.2M)

- MySQL 3.23.49 Benchmark/test suites (690K)

- MySQL 3.23.49 Development libraries & header files (1.2M)

- MySQL 3.23.49 Client shared libraries (231K)

For installation without using the RPM refer to the MySQL website.

The first two packages on this list are required for the basic installation of MySQL – the **Server** package will run MySQL as a background service and the **Client programs** package contains the classes to create, and manipulate, databases, tables and records.

Download the current stable versions of the **Server** and **Client programs** packages to any convenient location, such as **/usr/local**. These will be named something like **MySQL-3.23.49-1.i386.rpm** and **MySQL-client-3.23.49-1.i386.rpm**. Open a terminal window and navigate to the location directory then enter **su** at the prompt to assume superuser status ready to install the packages.

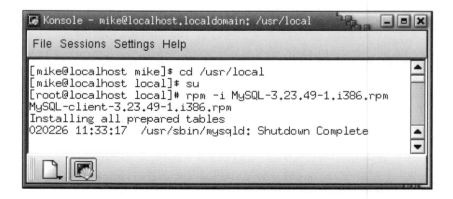

```
Konsole - mike@localhost.localdomain: /usr/local

File  Sessions  Settings  Help

[mike@localhost mike]$ cd /usr/local
[mike@localhost local]$ su
[root@localhost local]# rpm -i MySQL-3.23.49-1.i386.rpm
MySQL-client-3.23.49-1.i386.rpm
Installing all prepared tables
020226 11:33:17  /usr/sbin/mysqld: Shutdown Complete
```

Install both packages using the syntax **rpm -i *filename filename*** as shown in the illustration at the bottom of the opposite page. The MySQL server daemon will now be running and will be loaded whenever the system starts up. Its existences can be verified with the commands **mysqladmin ping** and **mysqladmin status** like this:

The MySQL server can be stopped by typing the command **mysqladmin shutdown.**

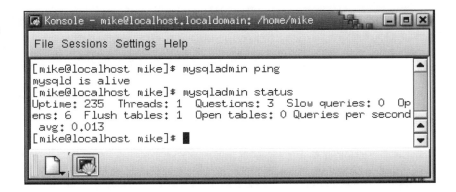

Type the command **mysql** to open the MySQL monitor where databases can be created and updated. Default databases called **mysql** and **test** are created during the installation process.

Type **exit** *or* **quit** *at the* **mysql>** *prompt to return to a normal prompt.*

Common SQL commands which are used to work with databases in the MySQL monitor are shown in chapter 11.

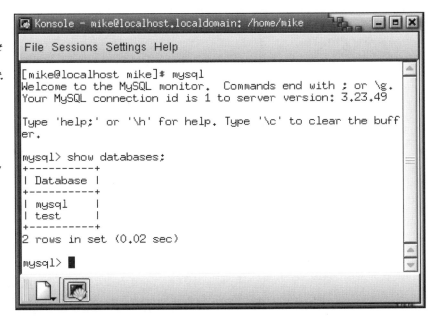

Installing Apache

Apache is the world's most popular web server which, according to a recent survey, accounts for 56% of all web servers worldwide. It can be freely downloaded from **http://httpd.apache.org** or one of the mirrors listed on that site.

Download the latest stable version to any convenient location, such as **/usr/local**. The file will be a tarball named something like **apache_1.3.23.tar.gz** that must be unzipped and the files extracted before installation can begin.

Navigate to the location directory then type **su** to assume superuser status. Now use **gunzip** to unzip the file and **tar -xvf** to extract the files, as shown in the screenshot below. A long directory structure will be listed in the terminal window before returning to a prompt.

*The first version of Apache, based on the NCSA httpd Web server, was developed in 1995. Because it was developed from existing NCSA code plus various patches it was called a patchy server - hence the name **Apache Server.***

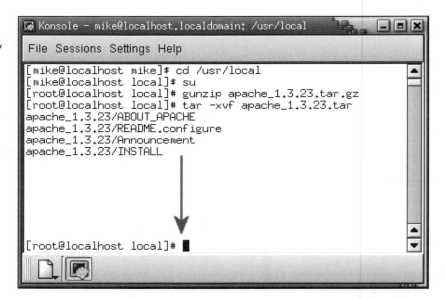

Extraction creates a sub-directory named after the Apache tarball, in this case its absolute address is **/usr/local/apache_1.3.23**.

Navigate to the newly created directory with a command like **cd apache_1.3.23** then run the configuration script with the command **./configure --prefix=/usr/local/apache_1.3.23 --enable-module=so**. This will now create the **makefiles**, needed for installation, before returning to a terminal prompt.

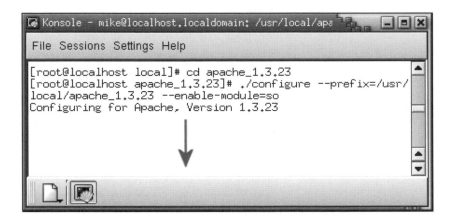

At the prompt type **make** then press **enter** to compile the installation files. When the terminal prompt returns type **make install** and press **enter** again to complete the installation.

Upon completion a declaration similar to the one below will be displayed in the terminal window to confirm a successful installation. The two further steps indicated in the declaration, to configure and start the Apache server, are shown on the next page.

Installation procedures may vary between versions. If the installation is not successful check the instructions on these pages then refer to the Apache installation instructions for your particular version.

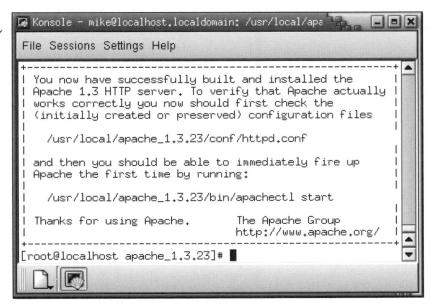

Configuring Apache

Before starting the Apache server for the first time two minor changes can be made to its **httpd.conf** configuration file. This is located within Apache's **/conf** directory with an absolute address similar to **/usr/local/apache_1.3.23/conf/httpd.conf**. Open this file in a text editor and find the section shown in the screenshot below:

*Read through the comments in **httpd.conf** to gain a better understanding of the Apache web server.*

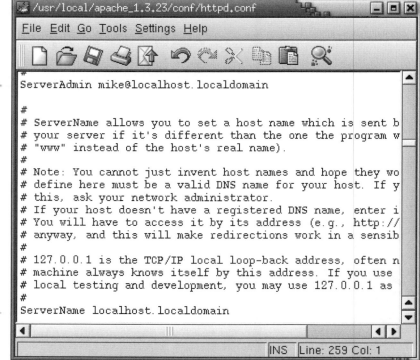

First edit the line beginning **ServerAdmin** so that it specifies your own email address. For instance, change the line to read:

ServerAdmin *yourname@yourmailserver.com*

Now edit the line specifying the server name by removing the **#** commenting character and change the name to **localhost.localdomain**, so the entire line looks like this:

ServerName **localhost.localdomain**

Finally, remember to save the file to apply these changes.

Running Apache

To start the Apache server navigate to the parent directory, such as **/usr/local/apache_1.3.23**, enter **su** to assume superuser status, then enter the command **./bin/apachectl start**. Apache will respond in the terminal window with the confirmation message **httpd started**.

*Apache can also be stopped by using the command **apachectl stop** in the Apache /bin directory.*

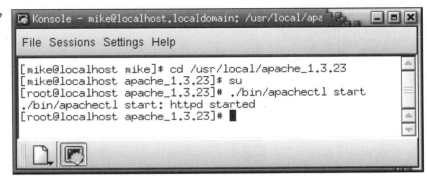

When Apache is running, a connection can be made from a local web browser by typing **http://localhost** in the browser's URL field. This will automatically search Apache's **htdocs** folder for a file called **index.html** which looks similar to the screenshot below:

*To have Apache automatically load during boot-up call **apachectl start** from a boot script. For instance, in Mandrake Linux 8.1 open **/etc/rc.d/rc.local** in a text editor and at the very end of the file add **/usr/local/apache_1.3.23/ bin/apachectl start**.*

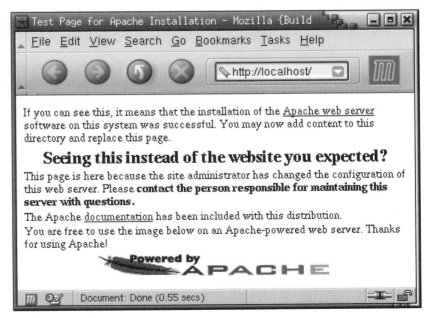

Installing PHP

The final component needed to establish a PHP development environment is the installation of PHP itself. The latest stable release can be freely downloaded from **www.php.net** as a tarball. This installation example uses **php-4.1.1.tar.gz** – the installation procedure may vary for other versions. This is first downloaded to a convenient location, such as **/usr/local**. This must then be unzipped and the files extracted before the installation can begin.

Navigate to the location directory then type **su** to assume superuser status. Now use **gunzip** to unzip the file and **tar -xvf** to extract the files, as shown in the screenshot below. A long directory structure will be listed in the terminal window before returning to a prompt.

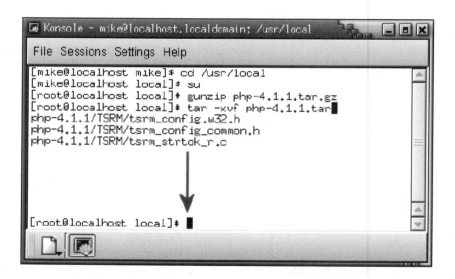

Extraction creates a sub-directory named after the PHP tarball, in this case its absolute address is **/usr/local/php-4.1.1**.

*Configuration uses **flex (lex)** and **bison** which must be installed as part of your Linux setup.*

Navigate to the newly created directory with a command like **cd php-4.1.1** then run the configuration script to include MySQL and Apache with the command **./configure —with-mysql —with-apxs=/usr/local/apache_1.3.23/bin/apxs**. Substitute the Apache location folder if the version is different to this example.

This process will now create lots of **makefiles**, needed for installation, before returning to a terminal prompt.

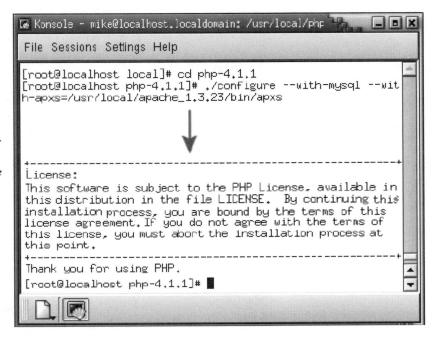

Each of these steps will produce lots of lines in the terminal as the installation proceeds.

At the prompt type **make** then press **enter** to compile the installation files. When the terminal prompt returns type **make install** and press **enter** again to complete the installation. When the terminal prompt returns PHP is installed on your system.

The installation includes a file named **php.ini-dist** that is located in the host directory, such as **/usr/local/php-4.1.1**. This is a template PHP configuration file that should be copied to **/usr/local/lib** and renamed as **php.ini**. For PHP versions later than 4.1.1. it is essential that you now open **php.ini** in a text editor and edit the **register_globals** configuration parameter to make it read **register_globals = On**. Installation should have automatically configured options for MySQL and Apache providing they were installed before PHP.

*For more about **register_globals** please refer to the notes on this book's*

page at:
www.ineasysteps.com.

The default configuration is for development purposes but an alternative configuration file, named **php.ini-recommended**, is supplied in **/usr/local/php-4.1.1** that provides on-line performance. Carefully study the notes inside this file before adopting it as your **php.ini** file and read the important security information available at **http://php.net/manual/en/security.php**.

Configuring Apache for PHP

Before the Apache server can run PHP examples it must be told how to recognize PHP file types. This is achieved by editing the **/usr/local/apache_1.3.23/conf/httpd.conf** configuration file to add the PHP MIME types to its list of recognized file types.

MIME is an acronym for Multipurpose Internet Mail Extensions which is a standard for defining file type formats.

Open the **httpd.conf** file in a text editor then find the section relating to the **AddType** instruction. Insert in the AddType section these two extra lines to identify the PHP mime types:

AddType application/x-httpd-php .phtml .php .php3 .php4
AddType application/x-httpd-php-source .phps

The file should now look like the illustration below. Save the file then restart Apache to apply the changes. When Apache encounters a file extension of **.phtml**, **.php**, **.php3** or **.php4** it will now run that file through the PHP parser before sending output to the browser.

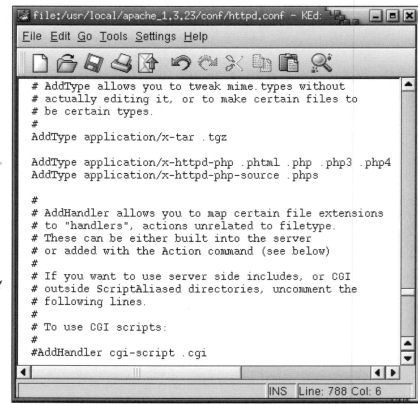

Refer back to page 25 for help on starting and stopping Apache.

Testing PHP

To create an initial PHP file that can be used to test the environment open a text editor and type this line of code:

phpinfo.php

```
<?php  phpinfo();  ?>
```

Save the file with the name **phpinfo.php** and place it in Apache's **htdocs** folder. This location is where Apache automatically looks for files that have been requested by a web browser.

▼ 📂 apache_1.3.23
  ▶ 📁 bin
  ▶ 📁 cgi-bin
  ▶ 📁 conf
  ▶ 📁 htdocs
  ▶ 📁 icons
  ▶ 📁 include
  ▶ 📁 libexec
  ▶ 📁 logs
  ▶ 📁 man
  ▶ 📁 proxy
  ▶ 📁 src

Now, with Apache running, open a web browser and type into its URL address field **http://localhost/phpinfo.php**. Press **enter** and PHP will generate the web page shown below, listing useful information about your PHP installation.

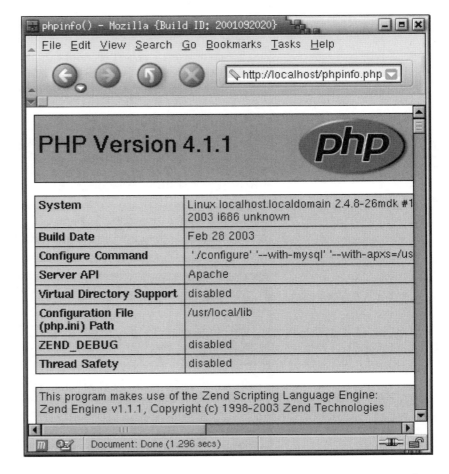

Testing MySQL connection

As a final test of the development environment a PHP script can be executed via the Apache web server to ensure that a connection can be made to the MySQL server running on the system. This will effectively involve all three components of the environment.

The test script is listed below within the HTML **body** section of a document. It will be explained in more detail later but, for now, it can be simply copied verbatim to check the MySQL connection. This document has been written in a text editor then saved as **mysqltest.php** in Apache's **htdocs** folder.

mysqltest.php

```
<html>
<head> <title>MySQL Connection Test</title> </head>
<body>
<h2>

<?php
  $connection = mysql_connect("localhost","root","")
   or die("Sorry - unable to connect to MySQL");
   echo("Congratulations - you connected to MySQL");
?>

</h2>
</body> </html>
```

When **http://localhost/mysqltest.php** is requested in a web browser address field the PHP parser executes the script code and a message will appear in the generated HTML output stating the test result. If the test succeeds the generated output looks like this screenshot:

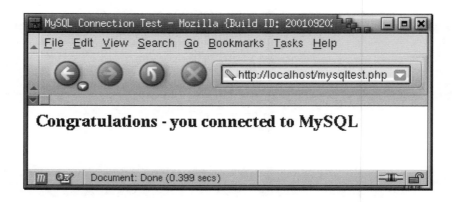

Getting started with PHP

All the examples that follow in this book are identical on both Windows and Linux platforms except that where file paths are mentioned they should be appropriate to the operating system. For instance, in Windows the Apache root directory for PHP files is **C:\Apache\htdocs** and in Linux the Apache root directory for PHP files is at **/usr/local/apache_1.3.23/htdocs**.

This chapter introduces the PHP syntax requirements and demonstrates how to use variables and functions.

Covers

Hello World | 32

Syntax rules | 33

Escaping characters | 34

Reserved words | 35

Variables | 36

Data types | 37

Functions | 38

Function arguments | 39

Multiple functions | 40

Variable scope | 41

Multiple arguments | 42

Chapter Three

Hello World

All PHP code must be included inside one of these three special markup tags that are recognized by the PHP parser:

```
<?php    PHP code goes here   ?>

<?       PHP code goes here   ?>

<script language="php"> PHP code goes here </script>
```

Probably the most common tag is the **<?php ... ?>** version that is used throughout this book, although the example code would be equally valid using either of the other two tag styles.

The most basic PHP instruction is the **echo()** function that is used to make the PHP parser dynamically write content into a generated HTML page. Literal content must be enclosed within quotes inside the function's parentheses and may include HTML markup tags.

In the simple example below the **echo()** function writes a traditional welcome message as a heading in a HTML page:

hello.php

```
<html>

<?php echo( "<h1>Hello World</h1>" ); ?>

</html>
```

This example is saved in Apache's **htdocs** folder so that the effect can be seen when the file is viewed in a Web browser, like this:

Because the **echo()** *function is so frequently used the PHP parser allows its parentheses to be optionally omitted.*

Syntax rules

PHP is not generally case-sensitive so the example on the opposite page could have been written like the following code and still produce the same result when viewed in a Web browser:

Normally use only lowercase characters for all PHP code.

```
<html>

<?PHP ECHO( "<H1>Hello World</H1>" ); ?>

</html>
```

It is important to notice the semi-colon at the end of the PHP instruction. This terminator must appear at the end of each PHP statement in the same way that a period must terminate each sentence in the English language.

Comments can usefully be added inside the PHP code block as explanation to third parties, or as a reminder when you revisit the code later. The PHP parser sees any text between //and the end of that line as a single-line comment, which it ignores. Alternatively single-line comments may begin with a **#** character. Also any text, on one or more lines, between **/*** and ***/** is ignored.

comments.php

```
<html>

<?php

/* Here is an introduction to this script code inside
    a multi-line comment block */

 echo ( "<h1>Hello World</h1>" );

// Here is single-line comment

# And here is another single-line comment

?>

</html>
```

When this example is opened in a Web browser, via Apache, the browser's View > Source menu option reveals only this code:

```
<html> <h1>Hello World</h1> </html>
```

Escaping characters

The \ backslash character can be used to apply special significance to the character that immediately follows it. This is especially useful to include quotation marks within a string of text to be written with the **echo()** function. As the string is itself enclosed by quotes the PHP parser would be confused by additional quotes and deliver an error message. This is easily avoided by preceding the additional quotes by a \ backslash character to escape them.

Single quotes or double quotes may be used to enclose strings.

Additionally the newline syntax **\n** can be used to move to a new line in text areas and **\t** will tab across the text area.

The following example creates a HTML text area containing text content that includes an escaped quotation and demonstrates the newline and tab features. The quotes containing the HTML attribute values for **rows** and **cols** are also escaped.

escape.php

```
<html>
<?php
echo("<textarea rows=\"5\" cols=\"48\">");
echo
  ("\"Utinam populus Romanus unam cervicem haberet!\"");
echo
  ("\n(Would that the Roman people had but one neck!)");
echo("\n\n \t\t\t Caligula A.D. 12-41");
echo("</textarea>");
?>
</html>
```

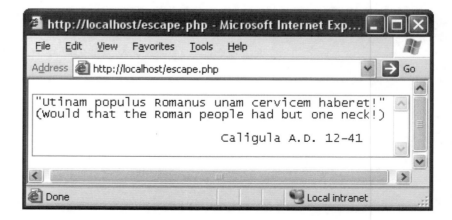

Reserved words

The table on this page contains words that are part of the PHP language itself. They may not be used when choosing identifier names for variables, functions or labels.

and	E_PARSE	old_function
$argv	E_ERROR	or
as	E_WARNING	parent
$argc	eval	PHP_OS
break	exit()	$PHP_SELF
case	extends	PHP_VERSION
cfunction	FALSE	print()
class	for	require()
continue	foreach	require_once()
declare	function	return()
default	global	static
do	$HTTP_COOKIE_VARS	switch
die()	$HTTP_GET_VARS	stdclass
echo()	$HTTP_POST_VARS	$this
else	$HTTP_POST_FILES	TRUE
elseif	$HTTP_ENV_VARS	var
empty()	$HTTP_SERVER_VARS	xor
enddeclare	if	virtual()
endfor	include()	while
endforeach	include_once()	_FILE_
endif	list()	_LINE_
endswitch	new	_sleep
endwhile	not	_wakeup
E_ALL	NULL	

Variables

A variable is a place in which to store data for manipulation within a PHP script. All variables begin with a **$** dollar sign followed by a meaningful name of your choice. When naming variables any letter, digit and the _ underscore character may be used but the variable name may not begin with a digit. These are all valid variable names:

```
$abc

$my_first_variable

$var123
```

Variable names are case-sensitive – so $var and $VAR are treated as separate individual variables.

Data is assigned to a variable using the **=** operator and the assignation statement, like all PHP statements, should end with a semi-colon terminator.

The example below recreates the text area example on page 34. In this case though the entire text content is assigned to a variable called **$str**. This makes the script more efficient because the whole text content is now written into the text area with just a single call to the **echo()** function, rather than the five calls used previously.

firstvar.php

```
<html>
<?php

$str = "<textarea rows=\"5\" cols=\"48\">\"Utinam
populus Romanus unam cervicem haberet!\"\n(Would that
the Roman people had but one neck!)\n\n \t\t\t Caligula
A.D. 12-41</textarea>";

echo( $str );
?>
</html>
```

Notice that the **$str** variable is not surrounded by quotes in the call to the **echo()** function because it is not to be treated literally.

Opening this example in a Web browser, via Apache, produces precisely the same generated page as that of the previous example shown at the bottom of page 34.

Data types

PHP is a loosely typed language so its variables can store different types of data such as numbers, text strings or boolean values. This is unlike programming languages, such as C++ and Java, that must declare a variable to be of a specific data type and may then only store data of the declared type inside that variable.

Data types that can be stored in PHP variables include:

- String – strings of spaces, text and numeric characters specified within double quotes ("...") or within single quotes ('...')

When assigning numeric values to a variable they should not be enclosed in quotes else they will be treated as string values.

- Integer – whole numbers without decimal places, such as 1,000

- Floating-point – numbers that do have decimal places, like 3.142

- Boolean – a truth value expressed with the case-insensitive PHP keywords of TRUE or FALSE.

Additionally a variable can be set to have no value at all by assigning it the case-insensitive PHP keyword of NULL.

vartype.php

```
<html>
<?php     $str = "Here is a string";
          $int = 77; $flt = 3.142; $non = NULL;
    echo("String:$str<br>");
    echo("Integer:$int<br>");
    echo("Floating-point:$flt<br>");
    echo("Null:$non");
?>
</html>
```

http://localhost/vartype.php - Microsoft Internet Ex...

File   Edit   View   Favorites   Tools   Help

Address 🔲 http://localhost/vartype.php   ▼ ➜ Go

String:Here is a string
Integer:77
Floating-point:3.142
Null:

🔲 Done   Local intranet

Functions

A function is a piece of PHP code that can be executed once or many times by the PHP script. Functions and variables form the basis of all PHP scripts.

PHP has lots of intrinsic functions, such as the **echo()** function, but you can create your own using the **function** keyword in a declaration. This is followed by a space then a chosen name for your function, following the same naming conventions used when naming variables. The function name is always followed by a pair or plain brackets then a pair of curly brackets containing the actual code that is to be executed whenever that function is called.

In this example the function has been named **go()** and it will write a short message and horizontal ruled line whenever it is called.

firstfcn.php

This example uses separate PHP elements to declare and call a function.

```
<html> <head> <title>PHP Functions</title> </head>
<body>
<?php function go(){
        echo("PHP adds dynamic content<hr>"); } ?>

<?php go(); ?>

<p>*** HTML is great for static content ***<p>

<?php go(); ?>

</body> </html>
```

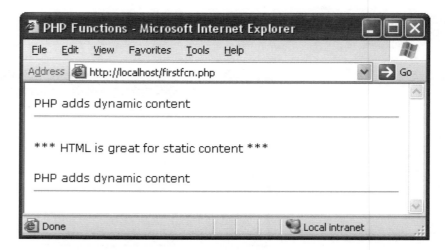

Function arguments

The plain brackets that follow all function names can be used to contain data for use in the code to be executed by that function. Just as the brackets of the PHP **echo()** function contain the string that is to be written in the generated page.

The data contained within the brackets is known as the function **argument**. In the following example the function call passes string values to the **go()** function's **$arg** argument for use in the code that is to be executed. In this case the string value passed from the function call is written out in bold underlined italic text.

arg.php

```
<html>
<head> <title>PHP Arguments</title> </head>
<body>

<?php function go($arg){
        echo("<b><u><i>$arg</i></u></b>"); } ?>

<p>This is the regular text style of this page.</p>

<?php go("This text has added style"); ?>

<p>This is the regular text style of this page.<p>

<?php go("PHP makes this so easy"); ?>

</body> </html>
```

Numeric argument values can be passed for manipulation by the function code.

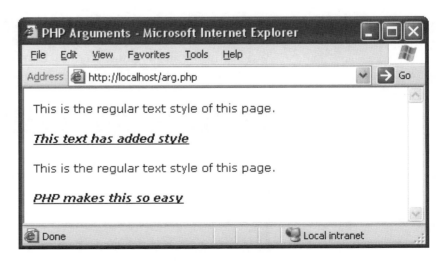

Multiple functions

PHP functions may call other functions during the execution of their code in just the same way that the previous examples called the **echo()** function.

The following example demonstrates the use of multiple functions to manipulate and display an integer argument value.

functions.php

```php
<?php
    function make_double($num)
    {
      $new_number = twice($num);
      echo("The value is $new_number");
    }

    function twice($arg)
    {
      return $arg + $arg;
    }
?>

<html> <head> <title>PHP Functions</title> </head>
<body>
  <h3> <?php make_double(4); ?> </h3>
</body>
</html>
```

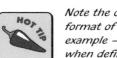

Note the code format of this example – when defining functions the source code is clearer if all declarations appear before any HTML or page content.

The argument value is passed from the calling statement to the **make_double()** function via the **show_number()** function. The passed argument value is doubled then the result is returned to a variable in the **show_number()** function. Finally the **echo()** function is called to write the new value out on the page.

Variable scope

Variable scope defines which parts of a PHP script has access to a variable. The variables used in the example on the opposite page are both declared inside functions so are known as **local** variables. These can only be used by the function in which they are declared.

Conversely **global** variables are declared outside functions and can be accessed by any function in that document. Unlike other languages which make global variables accessible automatically, PHP requires that a function must explicitly declare that it wants to use a global variable otherwise the variable will be deemed to be of local scope by default. A simple declaration inside a function's code block uses the **global** keyword followed by the variable name.

This example creates a global variable **$num**, made accessible to two functions by including a declaration in each code block.

scope.php

```php
<?php $num;

    function make_triple($arg)
    { global $num;
      $num = $arg + $arg +$arg;
      thrice();
    }

    function thrice()
    { global $num;
      echo("The value is $num");
    }
?>

<html> <head><title>Variable Scope</title> </head>
<body> <h3><?php make_triple(4); ?></h3> </body> </html>
```

Removal of either global declaration will render the code useless as PHP then assumes the variable reference in the function is made to a local variable.

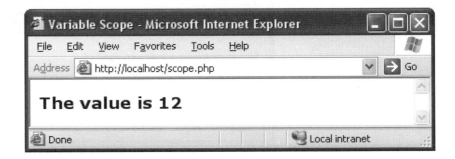

Multiple arguments

Functions may specify multiple arguments within their plain brackets to allow several values to be passed to the function code. The argument variable names simply need to be separated by a comma in a list.

When a function specifies single or multiple arguments all calls to that function must also normally include the correct number of argument values to avoid an error. Optionally a default value can be assigned to the argument in the function declaration.

In this example three arguments are specified with a default value to be used if no argument value is passed from the caller:

args.php

```php
<?php

    function addup($a=32,$b=32,$c=32)
    {
      $total = $a+$b+$c;
      echo("$a + $b + $c = $total");
    }
?>

<html> <head> <title>Function Arguments</title> </head>
<body>

  <h3><?php addup(8,16,24); ?></h3>

  <h3><?php addup(8,16); ?></h3>

</body> </html>
```

Function Arguments - Microsoft Internet Explorer

File   Edit   View   Favorites   Tools   Help

Address http://localhost/args.php   Go

8 + 16 + 24 = 48

8 + 16 + 32 = 56

Done   Local intranet

Performing operations

This chapter introduces the different PHP operators and demonstrates how they can be used in script statements to perform comparisons and to manipulate values.

Covers

Arithmetical operators | 44

Logical operators | 46

Assignment operators | 48

Comparison operators | 50

Conditional operator | 52

Chapter Four

Arithmetical operators

The arithmetical operators commonly used in PHP scripts are listed in the table below together with the operations they perform:

Operator	Operation	
+	Numeric addition	
.	String concatenation	
-	Subtraction	
*	Multiplication	
/	Division	
%	Modulus	
++	Increment	
- -	Decrement	

Notice that the **+** operator cannot be used to join together strings as it can in other languages. It will add together two numeric values and give the result of the addition. Concatenation of strings can only be performed with the . dot operator.

The modulus operator will divide the first given number by the second given number and return the remainder of the operation. This is most useful to determine if a number is odd or even.

The increment **++** and decrement **--** operators alter the given value by 1 and return the resulting new value. These are most commonly used to count iterations in a loop.

All the other operators act as you would expect but care should be taken to bracket expressions where more than one operator is being used to clarify the operations:

```
a = b * c - d % e / f ;          \\ This is unclear

a = (b * c) - ((d % e) / f );    \\ This is clearer
```

An example using the modulus operator to determine odd or even values can be found in the if statement example on page 54.

arithmetical.php

```php
<?php
    $addnum = 20+30;
    $addstr="I love "."PHP";
    $sub = 35.75 - 28.25;
    $mul = 8 * 50;
    $mod = 65 % 2;
    $inc = 5; $inc = ++$inc;
    $dec = 5; $dec = --$dec;

    $result = "addnum:$addnum  <br>";
    $result .= "addstr:$addstr <br>";
    $result .= "sub:$sub        <br>";
    $result .= "mul:$mul        <br>";
    $result .= "mod:$mod        <br>";
    $result .= "inc:$inc        <br>";
    $result .= "dec:$dec        <br>";

?>

<html>
<head> <title>Arithmetical Operators</title> </head>
<body>
    <h3> <?php echo($result); ?> </h3>
</body>
</html>
```

The increment and decrement operators may also be used following the operand. Note that in those cases they will perform the operation but only return the unoperated value.

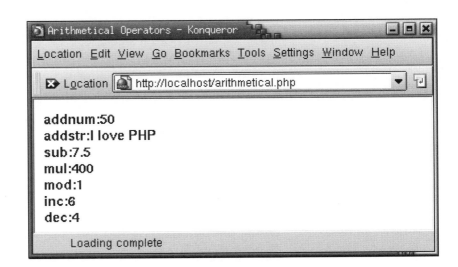

Logical operators

The table below lists the PHP logical operators:

Operator	Operation
&&	Logical AND
and	Logical AND
||	Logical OR
or	Logical OR
xor	Logical exclusive XOR
!	Logical NOT

The logical operators are used with operands that have the boolean values of true or false, or are values that can convert to true or false.

The logical **&&** and **and** operators will evaluate two operands and return true only if both operands themselves are true. Otherwise they will return false. This is typically used in conditional branching where the direction of a script is determined by testing two conditions. If both conditions are satisfied the script will go in a certain direction, otherwise it will take a different direction.

The **||** and **or** operators will evaluate its two operands and return true if either one of the operands itself returns true. If neither operand returns true they will return false. This is useful to perform an action if either one of two test conditions has been met.

The **xor** operator will evaluate its two operands and return true only if either one of the operands itself returns true but not both.

The ! logical **not** is a unary operator that is used before a single operand. It returns the inverse value of the given operand – so if a variable **a** had a value of true then **!a** would have a value of false. This is useful in PHP scripts to toggle the value of a variable in successive loop iterations with a statement like **a=!a**. This will ensure that on each pass the value is changed, like flicking a light switch on and off.

logical.php

To display the results this example uses the conditional operator that is described on page 52.

```php
<?php     $a = true; $b = false;

    #test both operands for true
    $test1 = ( $a and $a )? "true":"false";
    $test2 = ( $a and $b )? "true":"false";
    $test3 = ( $b and $b )? "true":"false";

    #test either operand for true
    $test4 = ( $a or $a )? "true":"false";
    $test5 = ( $a or $b )? "true":"false";
    $test6 = ( $b or $b )? "true":"false";

    #test for single operand is true
    $test7 = ( $a xor $a )? "true":"false";
    $test8 = ( $a xor $b )? "true":"false";
    $test9 = ( $b xor $b )? "true":"false";

    #invert values
    $test10 = ( !$a )? "true":"false";
    $test11 = ( !$b )? "true":"false";

    $result = "AND - 1:$test1 2:$test2 3:$test3<br>";
    $result .= "OR - 1:$test4 2:$test5 3:$test6<br>";
    $result .= "XOR - 1:$test7 2:$test8 3:$test9<br>";
    $result .= "NOT - 1:$test10 2:$test11";
?>

<html><head><title>Logical Operators</title></head>
<body>  <?php echo($result); ?> </body></html>
```

Assignment operators

The operators that are commonly used in PHP to assign values are all listed in the table below. All except the simple = assign operator are a shorthand form of a longer expression so each equivalent is also given for clarity.

Operator	Example	Equivalent
=	$a = $b	$a = $b
+= (for numbers)	$a += $b	$a = $a + $b
.= (for strings)	$a .= $b	$a = $a . $b
-=	$a -= $b	$a = $a - $b
*=	$a *= $b	$a = $a * $b
/=	$a /= $b	$a = $a / $b
%=	$a %= $b	$a = $a % $b

The equality operator compares values and is explained fully, with examples, on page 50.

It is important to regard the = operator as meaning "assign" rather than "equals" to avoid confusion with the == equality operator.

In the example in the table the variable named $a is assigned the value that is contained in the variable named $b to become its new value.

In the table example the += operator adds the numeric value contained in variable $a to the numeric value contained in the variable named $b then assigns the result to become the new value contained in variable $a.

The .= operator is most useful and has been used in earlier examples to add a second string to an existing string.

All the other operators in the table work in the same way as the += operator by making the arithmetical operation between the two values first, then assigning the result to the first variable to become its new value.

assignment.php

Using the .= operator with numbers will concatenate them – so that 8 .= 4 gives 84, not 12.

```php
<?php
    $a = "PHP "; $aa = "Script"; #assign string values
    $a .= $aa; #concatenate strings and assign to $a

    $b = 8; $bb = 4; #assign integer values
    $b += $bb; #add numbers and assign result to $b

    $c = 7.5; $cc = 2.25; #assign float values
    $c -= $cc; #subtract and assign result to $c

    $d = 8; $dd = 4; #assign integer values
    $d *= $dd; #multiply and assign result to $d

    $e = 8; $ee = 4; #assign integer values
    $e /= $ee; #divide and assign result to $e

    $f = 8; $ff = 4; #assign integer values
    $f %= $ff; #divide and assign remainder to $f

    $result =  "\$a ADD AND ASSIGN STRING: $a<br>";
    $result .= "\$b ADD AND ASSIGN INTEGER: $b<br>";
    $result .= "\$c SUBTRACT AND ASSIGN FLOAT: $c<br>";
    $result .= "\$d MULTIPLY AND ASSIGN: $d<br>";
    $result .= "\$e DIVIDE AND ASSIGN: $e<br>";
    $result .= "\$f MODULO AND ASSIGN: $f";
?>

<html><head><title>Assignment Operators</title></head>
<body> <?php echo($result); ?> </body></html>
```

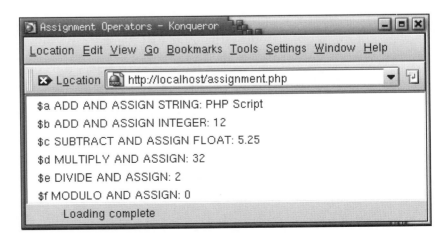

Comparison operators

The operators that are commonly used in PHP to compare two values are listed in the table below:

Operator	Comparative Test	
==	Equality	
!=	Inequality	
>	Greater than	
<	Less than	
>=	Greater than or equal to	
<=	Less than or equal to	

*An example of the **less than** operator < in a loop statement can be found on page 57.*

The **equality** operator == compares two operands and will return true if both are equal in value. If both are the same number they are equal, or if both are strings containing the same characters in the same positions they are equal. Boolean operands that are both true, or both false, are equal.

Conversely the != **inequality** operator returns true if two operands are not equal, using the same rules as the == equality operator.

Equality and inequality operators are useful in testing the state of two variables to perform conditional branching.

The **> greater than** operator compares two operands and will return true if the first is greater in value than the second.

The **< less than** operator makes the same comparison but returns true if the first operand is less in value than the second.

Adding the = operator after a **> greater than** or **< less than** operator makes them also return true if the two operands are exactly equal in value.

The **> greater than** operator is frequently used to test the value of a countdown value in a loop.

comparison.php

```php
<?php
    $a = ("PHP"=="PHP")? "true":"false";
    $b = ("PHP"=="PERL")?"true":"false";

    $c = (1.785==1.785)? "true":"false";
    $d = (5 != 5)?"true":"false";

    $e = (true == true)?"true":"false";
    $f = (false != false)?"true":"false";

    $g = (100<200)?"true":"false";
    $h = (100<100)?"true":"false";

    $i = (100<=100)?"true":"false";
    $j = ( -1 > 1 )?"true":"false";

    $result =   "TEST STRINGS \$a:$a  \$b:$b<br>";
    $result .= "TEST NUMBERS \$c:$c \$d:$d<br>";
    $result .= "TEST BOOLEANS \$e:$e \$f:$f<br>";
    $result .= "TEST LESS THAN \$g:$g \$h:$h<br>";
    $result .= "TEST LESS THAN OR EQUAL \$i:$i<br>";
    $result .= "TEST GREATER THAN \$j:$j";
?>

<html><head><title>Comparison Operators</title></head>
<body>
    <?php echo($result); ?>
</body></html>
```

To display the results this example uses the conditional operator that is described on page 52.

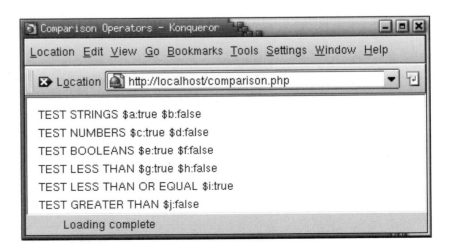

Conditional operator

The PHP coder's favorite operator is probably the conditional operator. This first evaluates an expression for a true or false value then executes one of two given statements depending upon the result of the evaluation. The conditional operator has this syntax:

```
(test expression) ? if true do this : if false do this;
```

This operator can be used to assign an appropriate value to a variable, as seen in some examples earlier in this chapter, or to call an appropriate function, as demonstrated in the example below.

conditional.php

Notice that each function uses the global keyword to make the $num variable value accessible – see page 41 for details.

```php
<?php
    function is_odd(){
        global $num; echo("$num is an odd number<hr>"); }

    function is_even(){
        global $num; echo("$num is an even number<hr>");}
?>

<html><head><title>Conditional Operator</title></head>
<body>
<?php
    $num = 57;
    ( $num % 2 != 0 ) ? is_odd() : is_even();

    $num = 44;
    ( $num % 2 != 0 ) ? is_odd() : is_even();
?>
</body></html>
```

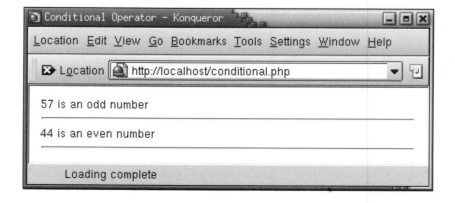

Making statements

Statements are used in PHP to progress the execution of the script. They may define loops within the code or be simple terms to be evaluated. This chapter introduces conditional testing and includes examples of different types of loops.

Covers

Conditional if statement | 54

If-else statement | 55

Switch statement | 56

For loop | 57

While loop | 58

Do-while loop | 59

Interrupting loops | 60

Return statement | 62

Chapter Five

Conditional if statement

The **if** keyword is used to perform the basic conditional PHP test to evaluate an expression for a boolean value. The statement following the evaluation will only be executed when the expression is true. The syntax for the **if** statement looks like this:

```
if ( test expression ) statement to execute when true ;
```

The code to be executed may contain multiple statements if they are enclosed in a pair of curly brackets to form a **statement block**.

In the example below the expression to be tested uses the modulus operator to determine if the value contained in the variable called **$num** is exactly divisible by 2. The statement block has two statements - one to assign a string value to a variable and another to call the PHP **echo()** function.

if.php

```php
<html>
    <head><title>If Statement</title></head>
<body>
<?php
    $num = 7;
    if ( $num % 2 != 0 )
    {
        $msg = "$num is an odd number.";
        echo( $msg );
    }
?>
</body></html>
```

This example could have used ($num%2!=1) to detect an even number.

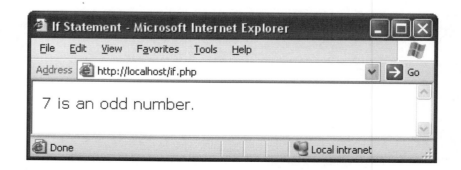

If–else statement

The PHP **else** keyword can be used with an **if** statement to provide alternative code to execute in the event that the tested expression is found to be **false**.

This is known as conditional branching and has this syntax:

```
if (test expression ) do this; else do this;
```

Several expressions may be tested until a **true** value is found when the code following the **true** expression will be executed. It is important to note any further code contained in the **if-else** statement is ignored.

In the following example, any code after the call to the **echo** function by the successful third test will be ignored completely:

ifelse.php

```
<html><head><title>If-else Statement</title></head>
<body>
<?php
    $num = 2;  $bool=false;

    if($num==1 and $bool==true) echo("Test 1 success");
    else
    if($num==2 and $bool==true) echo("Test 2 success");
    else
    if($num==2 and $bool==false) echo("Test 3 success");
    else
    if($num==3 and $bool==false) echo("Test 4 success");
?>
</body></html>
```

*The semi-colon is required after the first code statement before starting the **else** alternative code.*

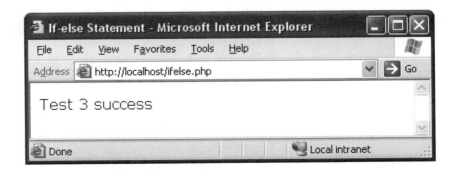

Switch statement

Conditional branching using an **if-else** statement can often be performed more efficiently using a **switch** statement when the test expression evaluates the value of just one variable.

The **switch** statement works in an unusual way. First it evaluates a given expression then seeks a label to match the resulting value. The code associated with the matching label will be executed or, if none of the labels match, the statement will execute any specified default code.

For more detail on the break statement see page 60.

The PHP **case** keyword is used to denote a label and the **default** keyword is used to specify the default code. All label code must be terminated by a **break** statement using the PHP **break** keyword.

The labels may be numbers, strings, or booleans but must all be of the same type, like this example which uses number types:

switch.php

*Omission of the **break** keywords allows the execution of all other code in the switch statement.*

```php
<html><head><title>Switch Statement</title></head>
<body>
<?php
    $num = 2 ;

    switch($num)
    {
      case 1 : echo("This is case 1 code"); break;
      case 2 : echo("This is case 2 code"); break;
      case 3 : echo("This is case 3 code"); break;
      default : echo("This is default code");
    }
?>
</body></html>
```

For loop

The **for** loop is probably the most frequently used type of loop in PHP scripting and has this syntax:

```
for( initializer, test, increment ) { statement/s }
```

The initializer is used to set the start value for the counter of the number of loop iterations. A variable may be declared here for this purpose and it is traditional to name it **$i**.

On each pass of the loop an expression is tested for a boolean result and that iteration of the loop will only run if the result is **true**. The loop will end if the test result is **false**.

*A **for** loop can also count down by decrementing the counter on each iteration with **$i--**.*

With every iteration the counter is incremented, then the loop executes the code in the statement. Multiple statements can be executed if they are contained by curly brackets to form a statement block.

The following example makes five iterations and changes the assigned value of two variables on each pass of the loop:

forloop.php

```php
<html><head><title>For Loop</title></head> <body>
<?php     $a=0; $b=0;
    for( $i=0; $i<5; $i++ )
    {
        $a += 10; $b += 5;
    }
    echo("At the end of the loop a=$a and b=$b");
?>
</body></html>
```

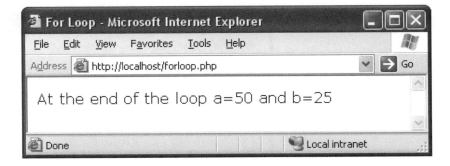

While loop

Another type of loop uses the PHP **while** keyword followed by an expression to be evaluated for a boolean value of **true** or **false**.

If the test expression is **true** then the code in the statement block will be executed. After the code has executed the test expression will again be evaluated and the loop will continue until the test expression is found to be **false**.

An infinite loop will lock the script so that the page will not complete.

The statement block must feature code that will affect the test expression in order to change the evaluation result to **false** at some point otherwise an infinite loop will be created.

It is important to note that if the test expression is not true when it is first evaluated the code in the statement block is never executed.

This example decrements a variable value on each iteration of the loop and the counter increments until it reaches 10 when the evaluation is **false** and the loop ends.

whileloop.php

```
<html><head><title>While Loop</title></head>
<body>
<?php     $i=0; $num=50;

    while( $i<10 )
    {
      $num--;
      $i++;
    }
    echo("Loop stopped at $i<br/> \$num is now $num");
?>
</body></html>
```

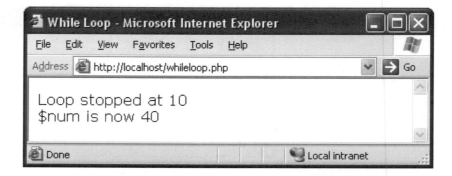

Do–while loop

The PHP **do** keyword is used to denote the start of a **do-while** loop and is followed by a statement block containing the code to be executed on each iteration of the loop.

The statement code is followed by the PHP **while** keyword and an expression to be evaluated for a boolean value of **true** or **false**.

If the test expression is true the loop restarts at the **do** keyword and will continue until the test expression becomes **false**.

It is important to note that, unlike the simple **while** loop, the statement code will always be executed at least once by the **do-while** loop because the test expression is not encountered until the end of the loop.

The following example will never loop because the counter value is incremented to 1 in the first execution of the statement code so the test expression is **false** on the very first time it is tested:

dowhileloop.php

```
<html>
    <head><title>Do-While Loop</title></head>
<body>
<?php
    $i=0; $num=50;

    do{ $num--; $i++; }
    while ( $i<1 );

    echo("Loop stopped at $i<br/>\$num is now $num");
?>
</body></html>
```

A while loop is often more suitable than a do–while loop.

Interrupting loops

The PHP **break** keyword is used to terminate the execution of a loop prematurely.

The **break** statement is situated inside the statement block containing the code that the loop executes and is preceded by a conditional test.

When the test condition is **true** the **break** statement immediately terminates the loop and no further iterations are made.

Notice in the output below that the counter value is still three because the increment in the final iteration is not applied.

In the following example the conditional test becomes **true** when the counter value reaches three:

break.php

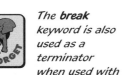

The **break** keyword is also used as a terminator when used with a **switch** statement – see page 56.

```
<html>
    <head><title>Break Statement</title></head>
<body>
<?php
    $i=0;

    while ( $i<6 )
    {
      if( $i==3) break;
      $i++;
    }
    echo("Loop stopped at $i by break statement");
?>

</body></html>
```

The PHP **continue** keyword is used to halt the current iteration of a loop but it does not terminate the loop.

Just like the **break** statement the **continue** statement is situated inside the statement block containing the code that the loop executes, preceded by a conditional test.

When the test condition is **true** the **continue** statement immediately stops the current iteration of the loop but further iterations will be made until the loop ends.

In the example below the test condition is **true** when the counter value reaches three so the string concatenation in that iteration is not applied but the loop continues on.

continue.php

```
<html>
    <head><title>Continue Statement</title></head>
<body>
<?php
    $i=0; $passes;

    while ( $i<5 )
    {
       if( $i==3) continue;
       $passes .= "$i ";
    }

    echo("Loop stopped at $i<br/>");
    echo("Completed iterations:$passes");
?>
</body></html>
```

The loop counter must be incremented before the **continue** condition is tested to avoid creating an infinite loop.

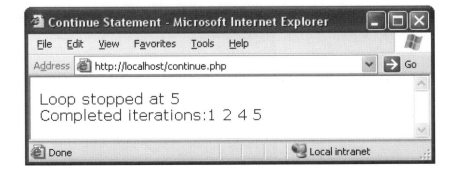

Return statement

The PHP **return** keyword is used in functions to return a final value to the caller of that function.

The example below contains a general purpose function called **multiply()** that can multiply up to five argument values and return the total to the caller.

It is called from within the **echo()** function to multiply three argument values. The total is returned, using the **return** keyword, and the echo function writes the total on the page.

return.php

*Each argument to the **multiply()** function uses a default value of 1 unless another value is passed from the caller. The example illustrated **returns** the number of minutes in a year, but the function call **multiply(365.25,24,60,60)** would **return** the number of seconds in a year.*

```php
<?php

    function multiply($a=1,$b=1,$c=1,$d=1,$e=1)
    {
      $total = $a * ($b * ($c * ($d * $e)));
      return $total;
    }
?>

<html><head><title>Return Statement</title></head>
<body>
Each year has 365¼ days<br/>
Each day has 24 hours<br/>
Each hour has 60 minutes<br/>
Each year has <?php echo( multiply(365.25,24,60)) ?>
minutes
</body></html>
```

Using arrays

This chapter deals exclusively with the topic of arrays and illustrates by example what they are and how to use them. The most useful special PHP array functions are demonstrated to show how to store and retrieve values in array structures.

Covers

Creating an array | 64

Changing array element values | 65

Listing array elements | 66

Getting the array size | 67

Adding & removing array elements | 68

Array keys and values | 70

One-based indexing | 71

Manipulating arrays | 72

Chapter Six

Creating an array

An array is a variable that can contain multiple values, unlike a regular variable that may only contain a single value. An ordinary variable is given array status by the PHP **array()** function. Multiple data values can then be assigned to array **elements** using the array's name together with an element index number. The index starts at zero and the number is placed inside square brackets, as seen here:

array.php

```php
<?php    $arr = array();

         $arr[0] = "First";
         $arr[1] = " PHP";
         $arr[2] = " array";

         echo($arr[0].$arr[1].$arr[2]);
?>
```

Each array element can now be used like a regular variable.

It is often convenient to specify the initial array values as a list of arguments to the **array()** function. This is demonstrated in the example below, which creates three arrays. The output from this example, and the one above, is shown at the bottom of this page.

array.php
(addition)

```php
<?php    $mo = array("Jan ","Feb ","Mar ");
         $dy = array("21 ","22 ","23 ");
         $yr = array("2003","2004","2005");

         echo($mo[1].$dy[0].$yr[1]);
?>
```

Remember that array indexing starts at zero. So $arr[2] is the third array element – not the second. See page 71 for how to create index numbering that starts at one instead of zero.

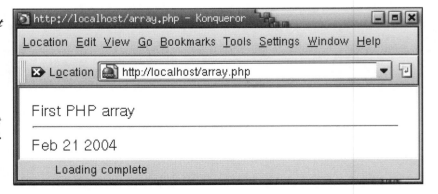

Changing array element values

PHP arrays are very versatile and each of their elements can contain data of different types within a single array.

To demonstrate this feature the following example creates an array that has three elements which initially contain string values. These are first written on the page using the **.** dot operator to concatenate the element values into a single string.

Next, new numeric values are assigned to each of the same three elements. The first element is assigned an integer value and the second gets a float value. The total of these is assigned to the third element with the help of the **+** addition operator. Finally the elements' new values are written out on the page.

chgarray.php

Array elements can also contain boolean values.

```
<html><head><title>Changing array values</title></head>
<body>
<?php
    #create an array containing 3 strings
    $arr = array("Red ","Green ","Blue ");

    echo($arr[0].$arr[1].$arr[2]."<hr/>");

    #assign new numeric values
    $arr[0] = 44;
    $arr[1] = 12.5;
    $arr[2] = $arr[0] + $arr[1];

    echo("$arr[0] + $arr[1] = $arr[2]");
?>
</body></html>
```

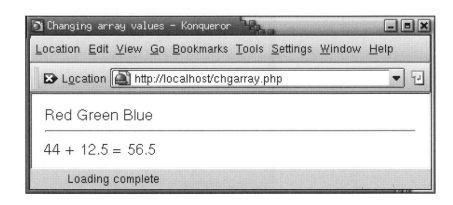

Listing array elements

Retrieving all element values from an array is easy with the PHP **foreach()** function that loops through each element of an array.

The value of the element on each iteration of the loop can be assigned to a variable using the PHP **as** keyword. This must be specified as an argument statement to the **foreach()** function that also states the array name and the variable name with this syntax:

```
foreach( array as variable ) { current variable value }
```

The following example loops through an array and writes each element value on the page as an item in an ordered list:

listarray.php

```
<html><head><title>List array values</title></head>
<body> <ol>
<?php    $arr = array("Red","Green","Blue",
                  "Cyan","Magenta","Black","Yellow");

    foreach( $arr as $value)
    {
       echo("<li>Do you like $value ?");
    }
?>
</ol> </body></html>
```

Getting the array size

The PHP **sizeof()** function is an alias for the PHP **count()** function so either can be used to determine the total number of elements in any array. These functions require the name of the array to be specified as their argument.

The PHP script below first creates an empty array then fills three elements with data using a **for** loop. Each of the element values are written out on the page using the **foreach()** function described on the opposite page. Finally the array size is assigned to a variable then written on the page.

sizearray.php

```
<html><head><title>Getting array size</title></head>
<body> <ul>
<?php
    $arr = array();

    #assign three element values
    for( $i=0; $i<3; $i++)
    { $arr[ $i ] ="<li>This is element $i"; }

    foreach( $arr as $value){ echo($value); }

    #assign the number of array elements
    $size = count($arr);
    echo("<li>Total number of elements is $size");
?>
</ul></body></html>
```

Notice that the array size expands dynamically to create more elements when needed.

Getting array size – Konqueror

Location Edit View Go Bookmarks Tools Settings Window Help

Location http://localhost/sizearray.php

- This is element 0
- This is element 1
- This is element 2
- Total number of elements is 3

Loading complete

Adding & removing array elements

Additional elements can be created at the beginning of an array using the **array_unshift()** function and elements can be added at the end of an array with the **array_push()** function. Each requires the array name followed by the element data as its arguments.

In the example below an array is created with just three elements. Two further elements are added at the beginning of the array then two more elements are added at the end of the array.

addtoarray.php

```
<html><head><title>Adding array elements</title></head>
<body><ol>
<?php
    $arr = array("Red ","Green ","Blue ");

    #add elements at beginning of the array
    array_unshift($arr, "Cyan", "Magenta");

    #add elements at end of the array
    array_push($arr, "Yellow","Black");

    #write out each element
    foreach( $arr as $value)
    { echo("<li>Do you like $value ?"); }
?>
</ol></body></html>
```

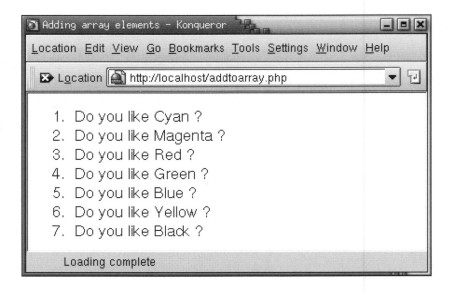

The first element in an array can be removed by the **array_shift()** function and the final element can be removed using the **array_pop()** function. Both these functions return the removed element data which can be assigned to a variable.

The following example removes the first and last element from an array then sorts the remaining elements into alphabetical order using the PHP **sort()** function.

fromarray.php

```php
<html><head><title>Remove array elements</title></head>
<body><ol>
<?php
#create an array containing 5 strings
$arr=array("Orange","Cherry","Apple","Banana","Lemon");

#remove element at beginning of the array
$first = array_shift($arr);

#remove element at end of the array
$last = array_pop($arr);

#sort elements alphabetically
sort($arr);

#write out values
foreach( $arr as $value){ echo("$value, ");}
echo("<br/>Removed first element: $first");
echo("<br/>Removed last element: $last");
?>
</ol></body></html>
```

Each of the PHP array functions in this example requires the array name to be specified as their argument.

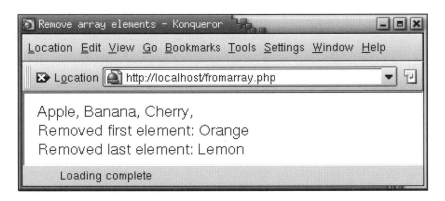

Array keys and values

In addition to single data content each PHP array element can contain **key-value** pairs where the **key** can be used in a script to refer to its associated **value**.

When assigning a **key-value** pair to an array element the **key** name, enclosed in quotes, should come first followed by **=>** characters then the **value** content. It is advisable to use single quotes to surround the **key** name to differentiate it from a regular string.

To refer to the **value** simply use the **key** name, in quotes, in place of the array index number, such as $arr['key'].

The example below creates an array with three elements containing **key-value** pairs. The element content is retrieved using each **key** to concatenate its associated **value** when it is written out on the page.

keyarray.php

Key names are case sensitive so $arr['OS'] and $arr['os'] refer to different array elements.

```
<html><head><title>Key-value array elements</title></
head>
<body><ol>
<?php
$arr = array( 'version' => 8.1,
              'OS'=> "Linux",'os' => " Mandrake ");
echo
("Platform:".$arr['OS'].$arr['os'].$arr['version']);
?>
</ol></body></html>
```

Data submitted from HTML forms takes the input name as a **key** and the input content as its **value**. These can be stored in an array so that user-entered data can be retrieved using the **key** name.

One-based indexing

By default the index of all array elements starts at zero, so that element number one is index number zero. This can be confusing but PHP does provide a way to start the index at one, so that element number one is also index number one.

The solution is to explicitly specify an integer key of one for the first element value using the **=>** syntax. All subsequent values will adopt successive index numbers which correctly match their position in the array.

This technique is demonstrated in the following example to make an array containing five elements be indexed as 1-5 instead of the default index numbering of 0-4. Each element value is written out on the page by a loop that can now conveniently refer to each element correctly by its index position.

1basedarray.php

```
<html><head><title>One-based array index</title></head>
<body><ol>
<?php
$arr = array( 1 => "1st","2nd","3rd","4th","5th");

for( $i=1; $i <= sizeof($arr); $i++)
{
   echo("Position $i - Element value: $arr[$i]<br/>");
}
?>
</ol></body></html>
```

Location http://localhost/1basedarray.php

Position 1 - Element value: 1st
Position 2 - Element value: 2nd
Position 3 - Element value: 3rd
Position 4 - Element value: 4th
Position 5 - Element value: 5th

Loading complete

Manipulating arrays

PHP arrays can be easily manipulated by the many special array functions. The **array_merge()** function allows two arrays to be merged. This requires the two array names as its arguments and adds the elements of the second array after those of the first array. A specified range of an array's elements can be selected with the **array_slice()** function. This specifies the array name and the start and end positions of the required elements. Array elements can be randomly rearranged with the PHP **shuffle()** function. The example below demonstrates each of these functions in action.

slicearray.php

A seed is first provided for the **shuffle()** *function by srand(). For more details please refer to the random number example on page 78.*

```
<html><head><title>Manipulating arrays</title></head>
<body><ol>
<?php    $arr1 = array("Alpha","Bravo","Charlie");
         $arr2 = array("Delta","Echo","Foxtrot");

    $arr = array_merge($arr1,$arr2);
    foreach( $arr as $value ) { echo("$value ");}
    echo("<hr/>");

    $arr = array_slice($arr,1,4);
    foreach( $arr as $value ) { echo("$value ");}
    echo("<hr/>");

    srand((float)microtime() * 1000000); shuffle($arr);
    foreach( $arr as $value ) { echo("$value ");}
?>
</ol></body></html>
```

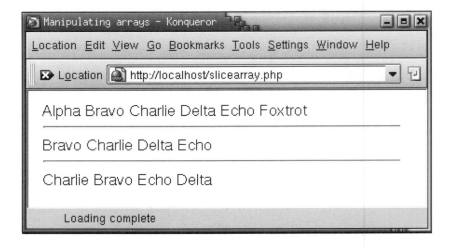

Generating dynamic content

This chapter demonstrates how PHP can provide dynamic content according to browser type, date and time, randomly generated numbers or user input. It also illustrates string manipulation and how the client browser can be redirected.

Covers

Identifying browser & platform | 74

Server date & time | 76

Time-specific content | 77

Random number generator | 78

Getting form values | 80

Displaying submitted values | 81

Manipulating submitted values | 82

String manipulation | 84

Reloading a page | 86

Browser redirection | 88

PHP and mobile devices | 90

Chapter Seven

Identifying browser & platform

PHP creates some useful **environment variables** that can be seen in the **phpinfo.php** page that was used to setup the PHP environment at the beginning of this book. These include an environment variable called **HTTP_USER_AGENT** which identifies the user's browser and operating system.

The script below uses the **getenv()** function to assign this environment variable then write its contents out on the page. The illustrations depict the script output in Internet Explorer on Windows XP and in the Konqueror browser on Linux:

identify.php

```html
<html>
  <head><title>Get browser &amp; platform</title></head>
<body>
<?php      $viewer = getenv("HTTP_USER_AGENT");
           echo("Browser details:<br/>$viewer");
?>
</body></html>
```

The details in Windows identify Internet Explorer 6.0 and Windows XP, as NT5.1. Also the Q312462 patch is installed here together with the .NET Common Library Runtime version 1.0.3705.

The information contained in the **HTTP_USER_AGENT** environment variable can be used to create dynamic content appropriate to the browser using the **preg_match()** function. This seeks to match a specified string pattern and has this syntax:

```
preg_match( "/string to seek/", "string to search" );
```

A match is sought to identify both browser and platform in the following example. Default strings are provided for when no match is found. The appropriate string is then written out on the page.

browser.php

```
<html><head><title>Browser content</title></head>
<body>
<?php    $viewer = getenv("HTTP_USER_AGENT");

    $browser = "an unidentified browser";
    if( preg_match( "/MSIE/i", "$viewer" ) )
        { $browser = "Internet Explorer"; }
    else if( preg_match( "/Netscape/i", "$viewer" ) )
        { $browser = "Netscape"; }
    else if( preg_match( "/Opera/i", "$viewer" ) )
        { $browser = "Opera"; }

    $platform = "an unidentified operating system";
    if( preg_match( "/Windows/i", "$viewer" ) )
        { $platform = "Windows"; }
    else if( preg_match( "/Linux/i", "$viewer" ) )
        { $platform = "Linux"; }

    echo("You're using $browser on $platform");
?>
</body></html>
```

*The **i** switch is included in the **preg_match()** first argument to ensure a case-insensitive search.*

Server date & time

The PHP **date()** function returns the current date and time on the server, formatted according to parameters specified as its arguments. The parameters are indicated by characters listed in the table below and examples are shown at the bottom of this page:

Character	Meaning
a / A	Prints "am" or "pm" / "AM" or "PM"
g / h	Hour in 12-hour format (1-12) / (01-12)
G / H	Hour in 24-hour format (0-23) / (00-23)
i	Minutes (00-59)
s	Seconds (00-59)
Z	Time zone offset in seconds (-43200 to 43200)
U	Seconds since January 1,1970 00:00:00 GMT
j / d	Day of the month (1-31) / (01-31)
D / l	Day of the week (Mon-Sun) / (Monday-Sunday)
w	Day of the week (0-6) from Sunday to Saturday
M / F	Month (Jan-Dec) / (January-December)
n / m	Month (1-12) / (01-12)
y / Y	Year (04) / (2004)
z	Day of the year (0-365)
t	Number of days in a given month (28-31)
S	English ordinal suffix ("th","nd","st")

```
$today = date("M j, Y");      # Dec 10, 2004
$today = date("m.d.y");       # 12.10.04
$time = date("g:i a");        # 5.25 pm
$time = date("H:i:s");        # 05:25:30
```

Time-specific content

The current date or time can be useful to create dynamic content appropriate for the day of the week, month of the year or the time of the day. The example script below writes a message appropriate to the time of the day at which the user accesses the server.

greetings.php

```
<html><head><title>Greetings</title></head>
<body>
<?php      $hour = date("G");
           $now = date("g:i a");

    $msg = "Good Evening.";
    if($hour < 18) { $msg = "Good Afternoon."; }
    if($hour < 12) { $msg = "Good Morning."; }

    echo("$msg The time is $now");
?>
</body></html>
```

*This script assesses an integer value of the current hour returned by the **date()** function. The message displayed may not be appropriate for users from other time zones.*

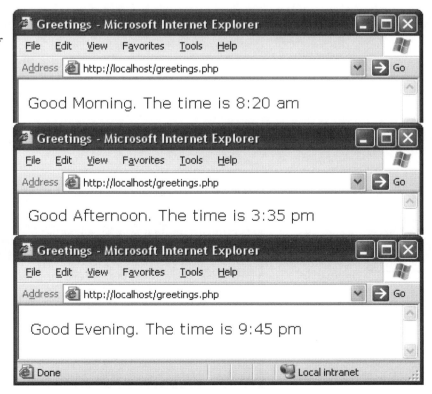

Random number generator

The PHP **rand()** function is used to generate a random number. Optionally a range of numbers from which the random number should be chosen can be specified as arguments to the **rand()** function stating minimum and maximum values of the range. For instance, **rand(1,10)** would select a number between 1 and 10. When no range is specified the random number will be between zero and the default maximum of 32767.

The random number generator should be seeded to prevent a regular pattern of numbers being generated. This is achieved using the **srand()** function that specifies the seed number as its argument. Commonly the seed number is specified as one million times the current time expressed to microsecond accuracy with the PHP **microtime()** function.

This example seeds the **rand()** function in the common manner then generates two random numbers in the range of 1 to 100.

random.php

```
<html><head><title>Random Numbers</title></head>
<body>
<?php
    srand( microtime() * 1000000);
    $num = rand(1,100);
    echo("Microtime:".microtime()."<br/>");
    echo("Random number:".$num."<br/>");
    $num = rand(1,100);
    echo("Another random number:".$num);
?>
</body></html>
```

The microtime has two parts – the second part is the number of seconds since 00:00:00 January 1, 1970 GMT, and the first part is the microsecond component.

The random number generator is useful to generate different banners on web pages so that the content can change on each visit. The example below generates a random number then selects a banner image, and associated hyperlink, according to the number.

randompix.php

The four banner images and link pages are located in Apache's **htdocs** *folder, alongside the* **randompix.php** *file.*

```php
<html><head><title>Random Images</title></head>
<body bgcolor="#000000">
<?php
srand( microtime() * 1000000);
$num = rand(1,4);

switch($num)
{
case 1 : $car="alfa.jpg";    $url="alfa.php";    break;
case 2 : $car="ferrari.jpg"; $url="ferrari.php"; break;
case 3 : $car="jaguar.jpg";  $url="jaguar.php";  break;
case 4 : $car="porsche.jpg"; $url="porsche.php"; break;
}
$banner = "<a href=\"$url\"> ";
$banner.= "<img src=\"$car\"   ";
$banner.= "width=\"380\" height=\"110\" border=\"0\" >";
$banner.="</a>";
echo($banner);
?>
</body></html>
```

In this case the random number chosen was 4 – so the Porsche banner image is displayed and clicking on it would take you to the Porsche page.

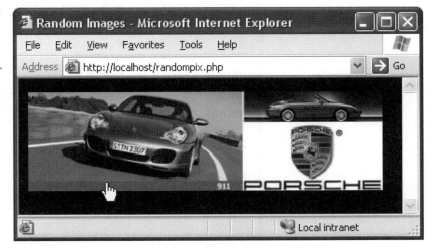

Getting form values

PHP is really good at handling data submitted to the server in HTML forms. Each type of HTML form input field sends the data as **key-value** pairs where the input name is the **key**, and the input field content is the **value**.

The simple HTML form shown below contains two text input fields called **username** and **dish** together with a set of radio buttons called **color**. Only one radio button may be selected at any time and its value will be sent to the server when the form is submitted.

fav.html

*Notice that the form's action attribute specifies a form handler named **fav.php** – this will process the data and is listed on the opposite page.*

```html
<html><head><title>Your Favorites</title></head>
<body>
<form action="fav.php" method="post">
<b>Please enter your first name:</b>
<input type="text" size="45" name="username"> <br>
<b>Please select your favorite color wine:</b> <br>
<input type="radio" name="color" value="white">  White
<input type="radio" name="color" value="rosé"> Rosé
<input type="radio" name="color" value="red"> Red <br>
<b>Please enter your favorite dish:</b>
<input type="text" size="45" name="dish"> <br> <br>
<input type="submit" value="Submit this form">
</form>
</body></html>
```

Displaying submitted values

When HTML form data is submitted to a PHP script for processing each of the form's input field names is created as a PHP variable. These variables contain the values entered by the user.

The PHP script below will process the form data illustrated on the opposite page. For the input fields named **username**, **color** and **dish** the script uses **$username**, **$color** and **$dish** to access the entered values. Notice that the script checks for a null value in each case to see that the user has indeed entered something.

fav.php

*The configuration parameter named **register_globals** must be turned **ON** in **php.ini**.*

```php
<html><head><title>Your submission</title></head>
<body>
<img src="foodbanner.jpg" width="368" height="54">
<?php

if($username != null)
{ echo("Thanks for your selection $username<hr>"); }

if( ($color != null) && ($dish != null) )
{
    $msg="You really enjoy $dish<br>";
    $msg.="- especially with a nice $color wine";
    echo($msg);
}
?>
</body></html>
```

*The first statement block will only be executed if the user has entered a **$username** value. The second statement block will only be executed if the user has entered both a **$color** and a **$dish** value.*

Manipulating submitted values

PHP can do much more than simply display values submitted from a HTML form. The submitted data is stored in PHP variables that bear the same name as each input field and these variables can be manipulated by the script, just like other variables.

The HTML form in the example below allows the user to enter two numbers then select an arithmetical operation to perform on them. When the form is submitted to the server these values are sent to a PHP form handler called **calc.php**, listed opposite. The data is associated with the key names of **val1**, **val2** and **calc** that have been used for the form's input fields.

calc.html

```
<html> <head> <title>Calculation Form</title> </head>
<body>
<form action="calc.php" method="post">
Value 1: <input type="text" name="val1" size=10>
Value 2: <input type="text" name="val2" size=10> <br>
Calculation:<br>
<input type="radio" name="calc" value="add">Add
<input type="radio" name="calc" value="sub">Subtract
<input type="radio" name="calc" value="mul">Multiply
<input type="radio" name="calc" value="div">Divide <br>
<input type="submit" value="Calculate">
<input type="reset" value="Clear">
</form>
</body></html>
```

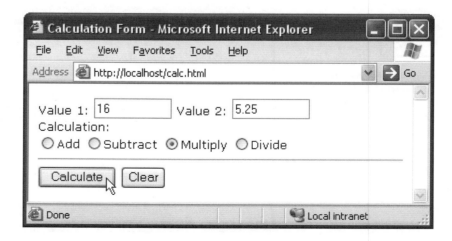

calc.php

```
<html> <head> <title>Calculation Result</title> </head>
<body>
<?php
if( is_numeric($val1) && is_numeric($val2) )
{
  if($calc != null)
  {
    switch($calc)
    {
      case "add" : $result= $val1 + $val2; break;
      case "sub" : $result= $val1 - $val2; break;
      case "mul" : $result= $val1 * $val2; break;
      case "div" : $result= $val1 / $val2; break;
    }
  echo("Calculation result: $result");
  }
}
else{ echo("Invalid entry - please retry"); }
?>
</body></html>
```

*The **switch** statement is seeking a match against the four possible values of the HTML form's radio button set.*

The form handler script above uses the PHP **is_numeric()** function to ensure that two numbers have indeed been entered. This function takes a value to be evaluated as its argument, and only returns **true** when the value is numeric.

If an arithmetical operation has been selected a **switch** statement determines the type of operation and performs the sum. The script then writes out the total of the calculation, or a request to retry if the user has made invalid or incomplete entries.

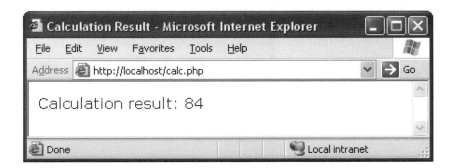

String manipulation

This example demonstrates how strings can be manipulated using some of PHP's string functions. The function name is sent to the server when the form is submitted as the value associated with the key named **fcn** by the **name** attribute of the form inputs.

strings.html

*The string to be manipulated in this example is the text input content of the textarea which is sent to the server with the **txt** key.*

```
<html><head> <title>String Manipulation</title> </head>
<body>
<form action="strings.php" method="post">
<b>Enter some text here:</b><br/>
<textarea name="txt" rows="3" cols="45"></textarea><br/>
<input type="radio" name="fcn" value="strlen">
Find the text length
<input type="radio" name="fcn" value="strrev">
Reverse the text<br/>
<input type="radio" name="fcn" value="strtoupper">
Change to all uppercase
<input type="radio" name="fcn" value="strtolower">
Change to all lowercase<br/>
<input type="radio" name="fcn" value="ucwords">
Make the first letter of all words uppercase <hr/>
<input type="submit" value="Manipulate">
</form>
</body> </html>
```

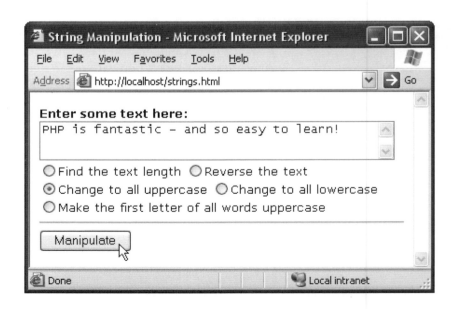

strings.php

```
<html><head><title>String Result</title></head>
<body>

<?php echo( $fcn($txt) ); ?>

</body></html>
```

The form handler script above takes the function name from the **$fcn** variable and specifies the string from the **$txt** key as its argument. The results of some of the manipulations are illustrated below for the string shown in the textarea on the opposite page.

*The **strlen()** function returns an integer total of the number of characters in a given string.*

*The **strrev()** function returns a given string in reverse order.*

*A given string is returned entirely in uppercase by the function **strtoupper()** or entirely in lowercase (not illustrated) by the **strtolower()** function.*

*The **ucwords()** function returns a given string with the first letter of each word in uppercase.*

Reloading a page

Previous examples have nominated a different file as a form handler to process submitted data but the same page can be used as the form handler by assigning the PHP environment variable called **PHP_SELF** to the form's **action** attribute.

The following example demonstrating this is a guessing game that generates a random number when it is first loaded and assigns it to a hidden form input. The page contains an initial code block that starts with a call to the PHP **header()** function. Its specified argument of **Cache-Control:no-cache** indicates that the browser should always reload this page, rather than use a cached copy.

Also the initial code block contains a function called **setnum()** that generates a random number between 1 and 20 and assigns it to a variable called **$num**. Later down the page this value is assigned to the hidden form input called **num**. When the form is submitted the page reloads and retains the value of the **$num** variable. If the user guesses the number correctly the script calls the **setnum()** function to assign a new target number to the **$num** variable.

guess.php

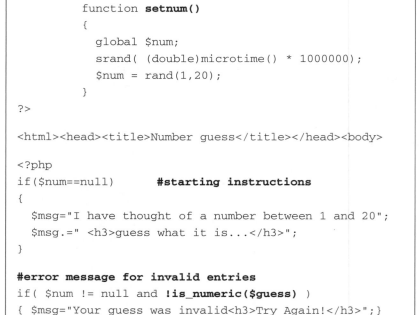

```php
<?php        header("Cache-Control:no-cache");

             function setnum()
             {
               global $num;
               srand( (double)microtime() * 1000000);
               $num = rand(1,20);
             }
?>

<html><head><title>Number guess</title></head><body>

<?php
if($num==null)              #starting instructions
{
  $msg="I have thought of a number between 1 and 20";
  $msg.=" <h3>guess what it is...</h3>";
}

#error message for invalid entries
if( $num != null and !is_numeric($guess) )
{ $msg="Your guess was invalid<h3>Try Again!</h3>";}
```

Notice that the syntax to check for non-numeric entries uses **!is_numeric($guess).**

guess.php
(continued)

```
else if($guess == $num)    #is guess correct?
{
  if($num != null)
  {
    $msg="CORRECT! - THE NUMBER WAS $num";
    $msg.="<h3><a href=\"$PHP_SELF\">";
    $msg.="CLICK HERE TO TRY AGAIN???</a></h3>";
  }
  setnum();     #set a number number to guess
}
else if($guess > $num)     #is guess too high?
{ $msg="You guessed $guess<h3>My number is lower!</
h3>";}
else if($guess < $num)     #is guess too low?
{ $msg="You guessed $guess<h3>My number is higher!</
h3>";}

echo($msg);                #write the message out
?>

<form action="<?php $PHP_SELF ?>" method="post">
<input type="hidden" name="num"
                    value="<?php echo($num); ?>" >
Guess:<input type="text" name="guess">
<input type="submit" value="Submit">
</form>
</body></html>
```

Because the target number is written as the HTML input value it can be revealed by viewing the source code in the browser.

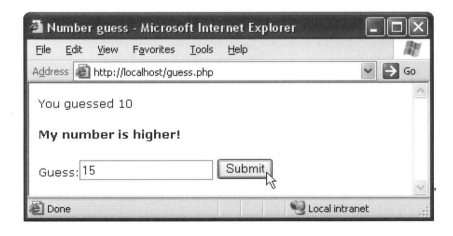

Browser redirection

The PHP **header()** function supplies raw HTTP headers to the browser and can be used to redirect it to another location. The redirection script should be at the very top of the page to prevent any other part of the page from loading.

The target is specified by the **Location**: header as the argument to the **header()** function. After calling this function the **exit()** function can be used to halt parsing of the code on that page.

In this example a drop-down selection box offers the user a variety of locations to visit. When the form is submitted the page is reloaded and the **$location** variable is used to redirect the browser.

redirect.php

The **header()** function sends a page header to the browser and must appear at the very start of the page, before any content is sent to the browser.

```php
<?php

    if($location != null)
    {
      header("Location:$location");
      exit();
    }
?>

<html><head><title>Redirect</title></head>
<body>
Choose a site to visit:
<form action="<?php $PHP_SELF?>" method="post">
<select name="location">
<option value="http://www.ineasysteps.com">
                                In Easy Steps</option>
<option value="http://www.amazon.com">
                                    Amazon</option>
<option value="http://w3c.org">
                      World Wide Web Consortium</option>
<option value="http://www.reuters.com">
                                Reuters News</option>
<option value="http://www.ebay.com">Ebay</option>
</select>
<input type="submit" name="submit" value="Go">
</form>
</body>
</html>
```

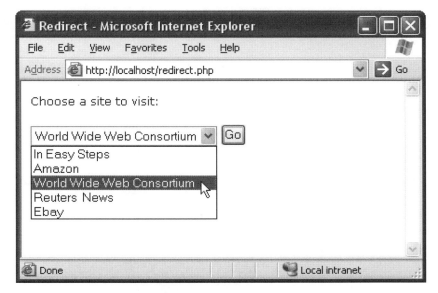

PHP and mobile devices

PHP can be useful to supply appropriate content to the emerging range of mobile devices that can access the Internet.

Commonly these have much smaller display areas than a PC monitor so large images are not suitable. Also they often have reduced capabilities and may not be able to read Web pages correctly. For instance, the **i-mode** standard favored by NTT DoCoMo uses Compact HTML (cHTML) which has only some of the tags available in HTML.

The example script listed below searches the **HTTP_USER_AGENT** environment variable to identify the browser. If it finds the **Pixo** micro-browser that is used on some mobile devices it will supply a small image. Otherwise a large image is supplied.

pixo.php

```
<html><head><title>Welcome Page</title></head><body>
<?php      $browser=getenv("HTTP_USER_AGENT");

if( preg_match("/Pixo/i", "$browser"))
{
  $img = "<img src=\"small-tux.gif\" ";
  $img.= "width=\"64\" height=\"75\" alt=\"tux\" >";
}
else
{
  $img = "<img src=\"large-tux.gif\" ";
  $img.= " width=\"320\" height=\"375\" alt=\"tux\" >";
}
echo($img);
?>

</body></html>
```

Alternatively PHP could redirect the micro-browser to a cHTML page containing content appropriate for the device.

File handling with PHP

This chapter demonstrates how PHP can read files and directories and how it can write new files on the server. It also illustrates how to copy, rename and delete files then shows how a script can upload files to the server.

Covers

Displaying directory files | 92

Copying & renaming files | 94

Deleting files | 96

Opening & closing files | 97

Reading a file | 98

Writing a file | 100

Logging visitor details | 102

Enabling file uploads | 104

Creating an upload form | 105

Creating an upload script | 106

Uploading a file | 107

Confirming file upload | 108

Chapter Eight

Displaying directory files

Special PHP functions can be used to display a list of all the files contained within any directory on your system. Before the directory can be accessed though, it must be opened with the **opendir()** function. This takes the full path address of the directory as its argument and returns a **directory handle**.

Path addresses for Windows locations must have double backslashes because the backslash is used in PHP for escaping.

Once opened, a loop can assign all the file names to a variable list using the **readir()** function to step through each file name. This takes the **directory handle** as its argument.

It is important to remember to close the directory when the loop has completed. using the **closedir()** function. Again, this requires the **directory handle** to be specified as its argument.

This example first assigns each file name in Apache's **bin** folder to a variable called **$file**, then adds them to the **$file_list** variable.

dirlist.php

*Notice how the loop checks for a **false** return from the **readdir()** function – after the last file name has been read **readdir()** returns **false** and the loop ends.*

```php
<?php
    #for Windows...
    $dirname = "C:\\Apache\\bin";

    #(for Linux... $dirname = "/usr/local/apache/bin"; )

    $dir = opendir($dirname);

    while( false != ($file = readdir($dir) ) )
    {
      if( ($file != ".") and ( $file != "..") )
      {
        $file_list .= "<li>$file";
      }
    }

    closedir($dir);
?>

<html><head><title>Listing directory</title><head>
<body>
<p>Files in <?php echo($dirname); ?> </p>
<ul>
<?php echo($file_list); ?>
</ul>
</body></html>
```

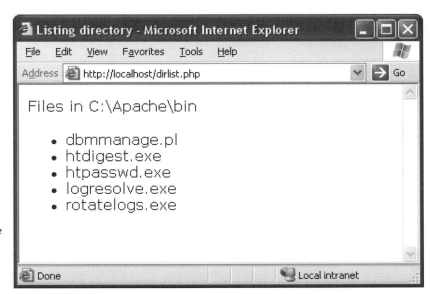

 *Adjust the code to have the appropriate path for your system. Note that the Linux version of Apache places more files into its **bin** directory, so a longer list is displayed from the **$file_list** variable.*

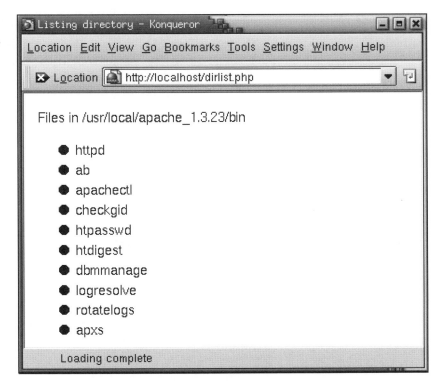

Copying & renaming files

Files on your system can be copied to any location using PHP's **copy()** function. This requires two arguments stating the full path of the source file to be copied, then the full path of the desired location where the copy is to be placed.

If the named destination file already exists it will be overwritten by the **copy()** *function.*

When the **copy()** function succeeds in copying the file it returns a **true** value, otherwise it returns a value of **false**.

The example below attempts to copy the error log file from Apache's **logs** directory then prints a message describing whether it succeeded or failed.

copyfile.php

```php
<?php
$source = "/usr/local/apache_1.3.23/logs/error_log";
$dest = "/home/mike/Desktop/error_bak";

# for Windows use...
# $source = "C:\\Apache\\logs\\error.log";
# $dest = "C:\\Documents and Settings\\All Users\\
                                Desktop\\error.bak";
if( copy($source, $dest) )
{ $msg = "Copied $source<br/>to $dest"; }
else
{ $msg = "Unable to copy $source"; }
?>

<html><head><title>Copying files</title><head>
<body>
<?php echo($msg); ?>
</body></html>
```

You must have correct access permissions for files to be copied – ensure that you have permission to write to the target directory.

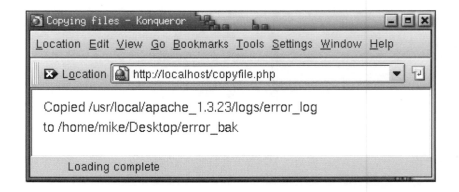

Files on your system can be renamed using PHP's **rename()** function. This function requires two arguments stating the original name of the file, then the new name to which it will be changed.

When the **rename()** function succeeds in renaming the file it returns a **true** value, otherwise it returns a value of **false**.

The example below attempts to rename the copy of Apache's error log file that was created in the example on the opposite page. Upon completion the script displays an appropriate message describing its success or failure.

renamefile.php

```php
<?php      $oldname = "/home/mike/Desktop/error_bak";
           $newname = "/home/mike/Desktop/errlog_bak";
# for Windows use...
#$oldname = "E:\\Documents and Settings\\All Users\\
                                    Desktop\\error.bak";
#$newname = "E:\\Documents and Settings\\All Users\\
                                    Desktop\\errlog.bak";
if( rename($oldname, $newname) )
{ $msg = "Renamed $oldname<br/>as $newname"; }
else
{ $msg = "Unable to rename $oldname"; }
?>

<html><head><title>Renaming files</title><head>
<body>
<?php echo($msg); ?>
</body></html>
```

*The **rename()** function changes the name of an existing file, whereas the **copy()** function creates a new file with the chosen name.*

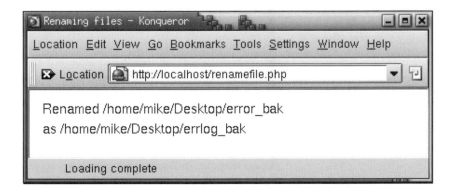

Deleting files

The PHP **unlink()** function permanently deletes the file specified as its argument if it is a valid file name.

In this example it appears at the beginning of the code in a custom function that attempts to delete a file then write a message confirming if the attempt succeeded or failed. This function is called twice later in the code to attempt to delete two files.

deletefile.php

```php
<?php function try_to_delete($file)
    {
      if(unlink($file) )
      { echo("$file<br/>has been deleted<hr/>"); }
      else { echo("Unable to delete $file<hr/>"); }
    }
?>
<html><head><title>Deleting files</title><head> <body>
<?php    $file_A = "/home/mike/Desktop/errlog_bak";
         $file_B = "/home/mike/Desktop/errlog_not";
         try_to_delete($file_A);
         try_to_delete($file_B);
?>
</body></html>
```

The attempt to delete the second file fails because the file does not exist. Warning messages can be suppressed by preceding the function name with an @ character in the function call. In this example, @try_to_delete($file_B); would suppress the warning.

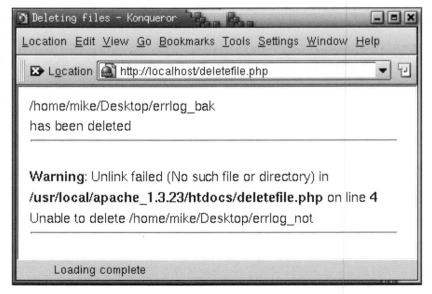

Opening & closing files

The PHP **fopen()** function is used to read text from files, write text to files and append text to files. It requires two arguments stating first, the file name, then a mode in which to operate.

File modes can be specified as one of the six options in this table:

The file mode characters represent **r** *for* **read,** **w** *for* **write,** **a** *for* **append** *and* **+** *for both* **reading and writing.**

Mode	Purpose
r	Opens the file for **reading** only. Places the file pointer at the **beginning** of the file.
r+	Opens the file for **reading and writing**. Places the file pointer at the **beginning** of the file.
w	Opens the file for **writing** only. Places the file pointer at the **beginning** of the file and truncates the file to zero length. If the file does not exist this will attempt to create it.
w+	Opens the file for **reading and writing**. Places the file pointer at the **beginning** of the file and truncates the file to zero length. If the file does not exist this will attempt to create it.
a	Opens the file for **writing** only. Places the file pointer at the **end** of the file. If the file does not exist this will attempt to create it.
a+	Opens the file for **reading and writing**. Places the file pointer at the **end** of the file. If the file does not exist this will attempt to create it.

If an attempt to open a file fails **fopen()** returns a value of **false**, otherwise it returns a **file pointer** which references that file.

After making changes to the opened file it is important to close it with the **fclose()** function to disconnect the **file pointer**. The **fclose()** function requires the **file pointer** as its argument and returns **true** when the closure succeeds or **false** when it fails.

The example on the next page demonstrates how to open a file, read the file, then close the file correctly.

Reading a file

A file can be opened with the **fopen()** function which requires two arguments specifying the file name, and one of the file modes listed on the previous page. The **fopen()** function returns a **file pointer** that references the file and can be used to read the file's contents.

The file can then be read with a function called **fread()** that also requires two arguments. These must be the **file pointer**, then the length of the file expressed in bytes.

The file's length can be found using the **filesize()** function which takes the file name as its argument and returns the size of the file expressed in bytes.

So the technique to read a file with PHP follows this pattern:

- open the file using **fopen()**

- get the file's length with **filesize()**

- read the file's contents using **fread()**

- close the file with **fclose()**

The following example assigns the contents of a text file to a variable, then displays those contents on the page.

readfile.php

```
<html><head><title>Reading a file</title></head>
<body>

<?php

    $filename = "/home/mike/Desktop/quote.txt";

    $file = fopen( $filename, "r" );

    $filesize = filesize( $filename );

    $text = fread( $file, $filesize );

    fclose( $file );

    echo( "File Size: $filesize bytes" );
    echo( "<pre>$text</pre>" );
?>
</body></html>
```

quote.txt

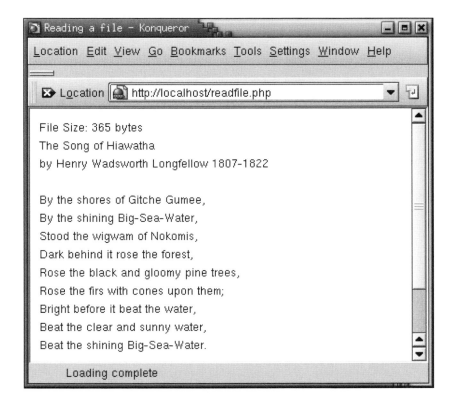

Writing a file

A new file can be written, or text appended to an existing file, using the PHP **fwrite()** function. This requires two arguments specifying a **file pointer** and the string of data that is to be written. Optionally a third integer argument can be included to specify the length of data to write. If the third argument is included writing will stop after the specified length (in bytes) has been reached.

The **file pointer** is obtained using the **fopen()** function with arguments stating the file name and one of the writing file modes listed on page 97.

After writing to a file it should be closed with the **fclose()** function that requires the **file pointer** as its sole argument.

The existence of a file can be tested with the PHP **file_exists()** function. This needs the file name as its argument and will return **true** if the file is located or **false** if it cannot be found.

The script below creates a new text file then writes a short text heading inside it. After closing this file its existence is confirmed.

writefile.php

```php
<?php
    $filename = "/home/mike/Desktop/newfile.txt";
    $file = fopen( $filename, "w");
    fwrite( $file, "Samuel Pepys 1633-1703\n\n");
    fclose( $file );
?>

<html><head><title>Writing a new file</title></head>
<body>
<?php

    if( file_exists( $filename ) )
    {
      $file_length = filesize($filename);
      $msg ="File created at $filename ";
      $msg.="containing $file_length bytes";
      echo( $msg );
    }
    else { echo( "Unable to create file" ); }
?>
</body></html>
```

This second script reopens the file created by the first script then appends a string to the existing heading. Notice that the mode specified to the **fopen()** function is **w** (write) in the first script but **a** (append) in the second script.

appendtofile.php

Note that these examples use /n to move to a new line and /t to tab across.

```php
<?php

$filename = "/home/mike/Desktop/newfile.txt";
$file = fopen( $filename, "a");
$string = "I went out to Charing Cross, to see Major-
general Harrison hanged,drawn, and quartered, which was
done there, he looked as cheerful as any man could do in
that condition\n\t\tOctober 13,1660";
fwrite( $file, $string );
fclose( $file );
?>
```

newfile.txt

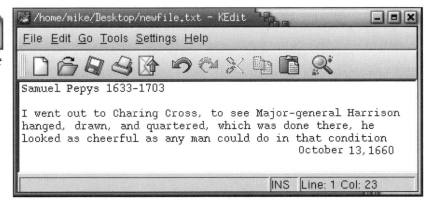

Logging visitor details

The ability to write files makes it simple for PHP to log details about visitors to a Web page and can help website development.

It is especially interesting to discover how visitors arrived at the page by recording the values within the PHP environment variable **HTTP_REFERER**. This holds the address of the page containing the hyperlink which the user followed to get to your page.

The frequency at which visitors return can be discovered by recording the IP addresses of visitors to a page that is stored in the PHP environment variable **REMOTE_ADDR**.

The following commented script demonstrates how to log these visitor details along with their browser type and the time at which they accessed the page.

log.php

The visitor may have typed the address directly into their browser, in which case HTTP_REFERER will not be set.

```php
<?
#open the log file
$file = fopen("log.html",  "a");

#write the time of access
$time = date("H:i dS F");
fwrite($file, "<b>Time:</b> $time<br/>" );

#write the user's IP address if available
if( $REMOTE_ADDR != null)
{
   fwrite($file,"<b>IP Address:</b> $REMOTE_ADDR<br/>");
}

#write the URL of the forwarding page if available
if( $HTTP_REFERER != null)
{
   fwrite($file,"<b>Referer:</b> $HTTP_REFERER<br/>");
}

#write the user's browser details
fwrite($file,"<b>Browser:</b> $HTTP_USER_AGENT<hr/>");

#close the log file
fclose($file);

?>
```

In this example the **log.php** file does not have any HTML content but in reality a regular page would be displayed. A variety of color-coded sample pages have supplied links to **log.php** and can be clearly seen in the illustration on this page.

Notice that the recorded details for the visitor using the Konqueror browser (next to the last entry) omits the referring page address as not all browsers recognize the **HTTP_REFERER** header.

log.html

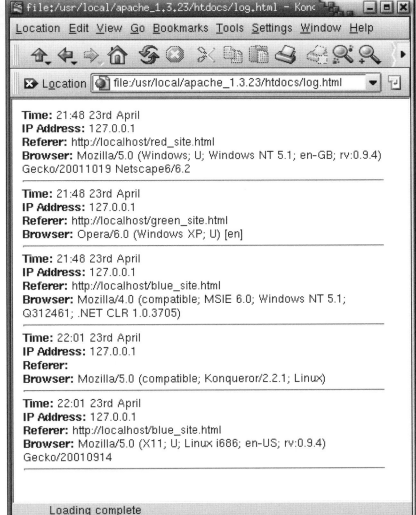

Enabling file uploads

A PHP script can be used with a HTML form to allow users to upload files to the server. The remainder of this chapter demonstrates how to create the upload form and the script to process that form.

Initially files are uploaded to a temporary directory then relocated to their target destination by a PHP script.

Information in the **phpinfo.php** page describes the temporary directory that is used for file uploads as **upload_tmp_dir** and the maximum permitted size of files that can be uploaded is stated as **upload_max_filesize**. The maximum default size is 2Mb and the temporary Windows directory is usually **C:\temp**. These can be modified by editing the **php.ini** file. In Linux the temporary directory need not be specified.

The process of uploading a file follows these steps:

- The user opens the page containing a HTML form featuring a text field, a browse button and a submit button

- The user clicks the browse button and selects a file to upload from his or her hard drive

- The full path to the selected file appears in the text field then the user clicks the submit button

- The selected file is sent to the temporary directory on the server

- The PHP script that was specified as the form handler in the form's action attribute checks that the file has arrived then copies the file to its intended destination

- The PHP script confirms the success to the user

As usual when writing files it is necessary for both temporary and final locations to have permissions set that enable writing – if either are set to be **read-only** the process will fail.

The upload file used in the example on the following pages is a image file in JPEG format but could equally have been a text file or any other type of valid file.

Creating an upload form

The uploader form is similar to the forms used in previous examples but with two important differences. Firstly, the form tag must include an **enctype** attribute with **multipart/form-data** assigned as its value. Secondly, the form must feature an input of the **file type** which puts a text field and a browse button on the page.

The HTML code below creates an uploader form with each of these features, along with a submit button.

uploader.html

```
<html><head> <title>File Uploader</title> </head>
<body> <h3>File Upload</h3>
Select a file to upload:<br/>

<form action="uploader.php" method="post"
                            enctype="multipart/form-data">

<input type="file" name="file" size="50">
<br/>
<input type="submit" value="Upload File">
</form>

</body> </html>
```

Notice that the form handler to process this form is the **uploader.php** script assigned to the form's **action** attribute – this is listed on the next page.

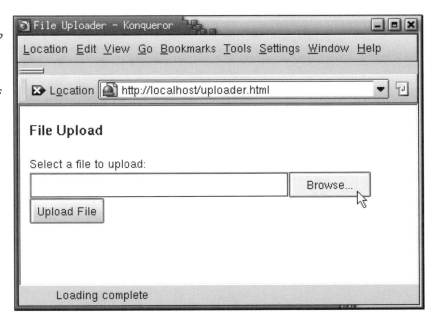

Creating an upload script

PHP automatically creates three additional variables for HTML **file** inputs that store information about the uploaded file. Their names are based upon the name specified as the input name suffixed with **_name**, **_size** and **_type**. So if the value assigned to the input's **name** attribute was **file**, PHP would create these four variables:

*   **$file** – the uploaded file in the temporary directory on the server

*   **$file_name** – the actual name of the uploaded file

*   **$file_size** – the size in bytes of the uploaded file

*   **$file_type** – the MIME type of the uploaded file

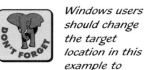

Windows users should change the target location in this example to
C:\\Apache\\htdocs\\ $file_name.

To accommodate the possibility that a file transfer may not complete successfully the PHP **die()** function can be used to terminate the execution of a script and display a string specified as its argument.

The example below attempts to copy a file uploaded by the HTML form listed on the previous page to Apache's **htdocs** directory and will display all the file's details upon completion.

uploader.php

```php
<?php
if($file_name !="")
{
copy ("$file", "/usr/local/apache_1.3.23/$file_name")
    or die("Could not copy file");
}
else { die("No file specified"); }
?>
<html><head> <title>Upload complete</title> </head>
<body> <h3>File upload succeeded...</h3>
<ul>
<li>Sent: <?php echo "$file_name"; ?>
<li>Size: <?php echo "$file_size"; ?> bytes
<li>Type: <?php echo "$file_type"; ?>
</ul>
<a href="<?php echo "$file_name" ?>">
                    Click here to view file</a>
</body>
</html>
```

This script also provides a hyperlink which can load the uploaded file into the browser.

Uploading a file

Browse to select a file to upload, click on the OK button, then push the form's submit button to upload that file to the server.

Confirming file upload

When the file has been uploaded confirmation details are displayed and the user can click the hyperlink to view the uploaded file.

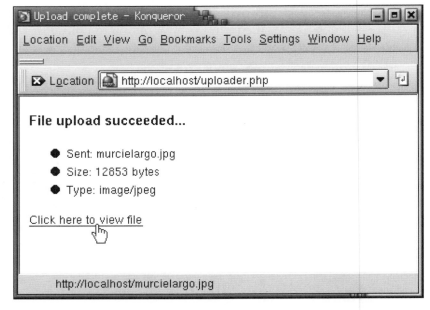

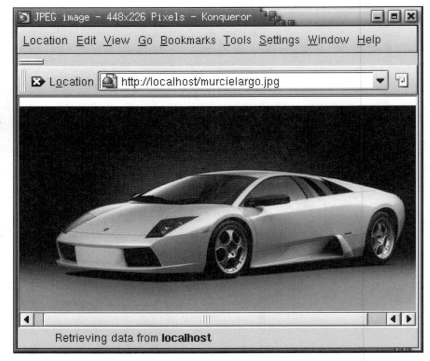

Data persistence

This chapter demonstrates how data can be stored by PHP so that it remains accessible as the user navigates around the various pages of a website. Examples illustrate two possible techniques, employing **cookies** and **session variables**. The advantages of each technique are examined.

Covers

Introducing cookies | 110

Set a cookie | 112

Access limitation | 114

Introducing sessions | 116

Starting a session | 118

Sessions without cookies | 120

Setting session preferences | 122

Cookies or sessions? | 124

Chapter Nine

Introducing cookies

Cookies are text files stored on the client computer that can each contain around 4000 characters. Up to 20 cookies can be stored for each website, and the client computer can store a maximum of 300 cookies in total.

Cookie files can be opened with any text editor so sensitive information should be encrypted. They are useful to retain user preferences, shopping cart selections, and other snippets of data. For instance, rather than directly store a user's password in a cookie it is better to store a unique identification string that references a database entry containing the password on the server.

When a user has logged onto a site their first name could be stored in a cookie so that each page they visit could greet them by name.

In PHP cookies are created with the **setcookie()** function. It is important to remember that this must appear on the page before any other code because a cookie is part of the header information. Failing to follow this rule causes an error like the example below:

nocookie.php

```
<html>
<head> <title>Invalid cookie</title> </head>
<body>

<?php
    setcookie("not","good","","/","",0);
?>

</body></html>
```

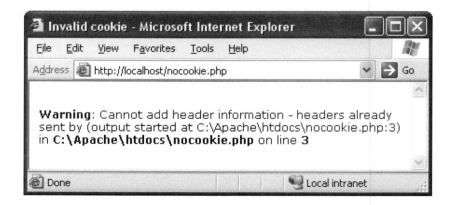

The **setcookie()** function sets just one cookie at a time and requires up to six arguments. These are described in the following list, in the order in which they must appear:

- **Name** - This sets the name of the cookie and is stored in an environment variable called HTTP_COOKIE_VARS. This named variable will be accessible to subsequent PHP page scripts.

- **Value** - This sets the value of the named variable and is the content that you actually want to store.

*The **setcookie()** function can be used with an expiry date in the past to delete a cookie.*

- **Expiry** - This specifies a future time, in seconds since 00:00:00 GMT on 1st January, 1970, at which the cookie will become inaccessible. If this argument is not explicitly set the cookie will automatically expire when the Web browser is closed.

- **Path** - This specifies the directories for which the cookie is valid. A single forward slash character permits the cookie to be valid for all directories on the server. If a directory is explicitly specified then the cookie is only valid for pages within that directory.

- **Domain** - This can be used to specify the domain name in very large domains and must contain at least two periods to be valid. If this argument is not explicitly specified the default value is the host name of the server that created the cookie. All cookies are only valid for the host and domain which created them.

*The **expiry** and **security** arguments must be integer values. Other arguments can be replaced with an empty string if they are not to be explicitly set.*

- **Security** - This can be set to 1 to specify that the cookie should only be sent by secure transmission using HTTPS , otherwise if set to 0 the cookie can be sent by regular HTTP.

All the arguments except the **name** argument are optional. If only the name argument is present, the cookie by that name will be deleted from the user's computer.

The expiry argument is easily set by adding a number of seconds onto the current time, retrieved using the PHP **time()** function. Each of these examples would set a cookie named **ID**, with a value of **X12345**, to expire 24 hours after it is generated:

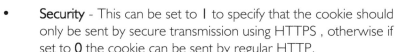

```
setcookie( "ID", "X12345", time()+86400 , "/", "", 0 );
setcookie( "ID", "X12345", time()+86400 );
```

Set a cookie

Once a cookie has been set its value can be easily retrieved in PHP simply by referencing the cookie name as a PHP variable. For instance, the value of a cookie called **data** can be retrieved in PHP scripts from the variable called **$data**.

It is important to remember though that the values stored in a cookie cannot be retrieved until the browser makes another HTTP request. That normally means that cookie values stored on page 1 can only be retrieved on subsequent pages in the website.

The following example demonstrates how to store two items of data entered by the user into form fields called **user** and **color**. When the form is submitted the page reloads. If values have been entered into both form fields the script stores these values in cookies called **firstname** and **fontcolor** respectively. The browser is then redirected to another page, listed opposite, which retrieves the stored values from within the cookies.

setcookie.php

```php
<?php
if( ($user != null) and ($color != null) )
{
   setcookie( "firstname",  $user,   time()+2592000 );
   setcookie( "fontcolor", $color, time()+2592000 );
   header("Location:getcookie.php" );
   exit();
}
?>

<html><head><title>Set Cookie Data</title></head> <body>
<form action="<?php echo($PHP_SELF); ?>" method="post">

Please enter your first name:
<input type="text" name="user"> <br> <br>

Please choose your favorite font color: <br>
<input type="radio" name="color" value ="#FF0000">Red
<input type="radio" name="color" value ="#00FF00">Green
<input type="radio" name="color" value ="#0000FF">Blue
<br> <br> <input type="submit" value="submit">
</form>
</body></html>
```

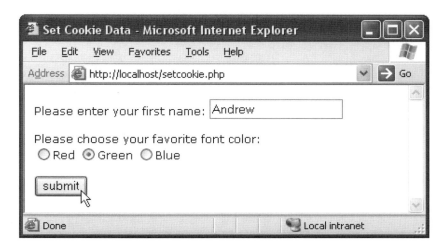

The second page gets the user's preferred font color from the cookie named **fontcolor** and sets the page text to that color in the style sheet. Also the user's name is retrieved from the cookie named **firstname** then written out on the page.

getcookie.php

```html
<html>
  <head>
    <title>Get Cookie Data</title>
      <style type="text/css">
        body { color: <?php echo( $fontcolor ); ?> }
      </style>
  </head>
  <body>
    <h1>Hello <?php echo( $firstname ); ?>! </h1>
  </body>
</html>
```

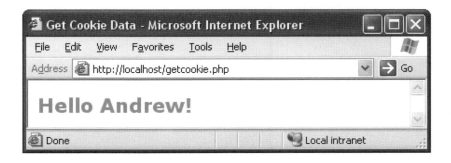

Access limitation

Cookies can be used to prevent direct access to pages of a website without having first logged in to that site. The log-in process creates the cookie, then PHP scripts on all other pages confirm the existence of that cookie before displaying their content.

In this example the log-in page creates a cookie called **auth** with a value of **ok** when the user submits the form with both **user** and **pass** input fields completed. The browser is redirected to a second page that seeks the cookie. If that page does not find the cookie the browser is redirected to the log-in page. Another page in this example executes the same check, and makes the same response.

login.php

```php
<?php    if( ($user != null) and ($pass != null) )
         {
             setcookie("auth","ok");
             header("Location:loggedin.php" );   exit();
         }
?>
<html> <head><title>Set Cookie Data</title></head>
<body>
<form action="<?php echo($PHP_SELF); ?>" method="post">
Name:    <br/><input type="text" name="user"><br/><br/>
Password:<br/><input type="text" name="pass"><br/><br/>
<input type="submit" value="Log Me In">
</form> </body></html>
```

This example makes no attempt to authenticate user name or password – authentication is illustrated in chapter 13.

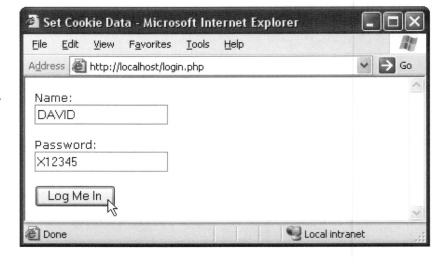

...cont'd

loggedin.php

```php
<?php       header("Cache-Control:no-cache");

if( ! $auth == "ok" )
{ header("Location:login.php" ); exit(); }
?>
<html> <head><title>Logged In</title></head>
<body>You are logged in and can access all pages on this
web site.<br><a href="anotherpage.php">Visit another page
on this site</a>
</body></html>
```

When you first open a browser **loggedin.php** *and* **anotherpage.php** *cannot be displayed unless you have reached them via the log-in page.*

anotherpage.php

```php
<?php       header("Cache-Control:no-cache");

if( ! $auth == "ok" )
{ header("Location:login.php" ); exit(); }
?>
<html> <head><title>Still Logged In</title></head>
       <body>You are still logged in... </body> </html>
```

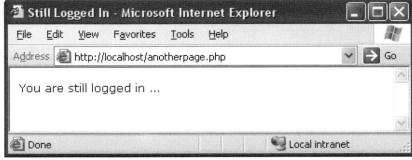

Introducing sessions

An alternative way to make data accessible across the various pages of an entire website is to use a PHP session.

A session creates a file in a temporary directory on the server where registered session variables, and their values, can be stored. This data will be available to all pages on the site during that visit.

The location of the temporary file is determined by a setting in the **php.ini** file called **session.save_path**. Its current value is shown in the session block of the **phpinfo.php** page and will probably be set to **C:\Windows\temp** on Windows or **/tmp** on Linux systems. The **php.ini** file can be edited to use a different location if preferred.

When a session is started a number of things happen:

- PHP first creates a unique identifier for that particular session which is a random string of 32 hexadecimal numbers, such as **3b4f0535c2dd9825df0bc2fc937e3443**

- A cookie called **PHPSESSID** is automatically sent to the user's computer to store the unique session identification string

- A file is automatically created on the server, in the designated temporary directory, and bears the name of the unique identifier prefixed by **sess_(sess_3b4f0535c2dd9825df0bc2fc937e3443)**

Now that the session is established data can be stored in registered session variables that are recorded in the file on the server within the temporary directory.

When the browser closes, or when the session is terminated, the **PHPSESSID** *cookie is automatically deleted.*

When a script wants to retrieve the value from a session variable PHP automatically gets the unique session identifier string from the **PHPSESSID** cookie, then looks in its temporary directory for the file bearing that name. Once this is located the file is opened and the value of the variable is recovered.

As this process relies only upon the cookie on the user's computer and the file in the server's temporary directory the session variables are available to each page of the entire site.

The session ends when the user closes their browser or, after leaving the site, the server will terminate the session after a predetermined period of time, commonly 30 minutes duration.

Netscape and Mozilla Web browsers have an excellent **Cookie Manager** facility that enables you to easily view the cookies stored on your computer. This can be used to verify the existence of a session cookie when a PHP session has been started.

A session must be started before you can find a **PHPSESSID** *cookie - starting a session is described on the next page.*

In the Netscape/Mozilla browser window click **Edit** on the taskbar then choose **Preferences** from the menu to open the **Preferences** dialog box. Select the **Privacy & Security** category then click on **Cookies** in the sub-menu to reveal the **Cookie Acceptance Policy** settings. In that dialog box click the button marked **View Stored Cookies** to open the **Cookie Manager** dialog box.

Selecting the **PHPSESSID** cookie reveals the data it contains in the dialog box's **Information** field, as shown in the illustration below:

The data in the **PHPSESSID** *cookie shown here matches this file created in the temporary directory:*

sess_3b4f053
5c2dd9825df0
bc2fc937e344
3

Cookie Manager ⊠

| Stored Cookies | Cookie Sites |

View and Remove Cookies that are stored on your computer.

Site	Cookie Name
localhost	PHPSESSID

Information about the selected Cookie

Name:	PHPSESSID
Information:	3b4f0535c2dd9825df0bc2fc937e3443
Host:	localhost
Path:	/
Server Secure:	no
Expires:	at end of session

[Remove Cookie]   [Remove All Cookies]

☐ Don't allow removed cookies to be reaccepted later

[OK]   [Cancel]

Starting a session

A PHP session is easily started by making a call to the **session_start()** function. This first checks to see if a session has already been started, then starts one if none currently exists. It also alerts the PHP engine to expect session variables to be used in the scripts on this page. It is therefore recommended to put the call to **session_start()** at the beginning of the page.

Session variables are **registered** with the **session_register()** function that takes the variable name as its argument.

The following example starts a session then registers a variable called **count** that is incremented each time the page is visited during the session.

count.php

```php
<?php      #start a session
           session_start();

           #register a session variable called count
           session_register("count");

           #increment the value of the counter variable
           $count++;
?>
<html><head><title>Count visits</title></head>
<body>

<?php
    #display the current value of the count variable
    $msg = "You have visited this page $count times ";
    $msg.= "in this session.";
    echo( $msg );
?>

</body></html>
```

*Set the option to warn before accepting cookies in order to see when the **PHPSESSID** cookie is sent to the browser.*

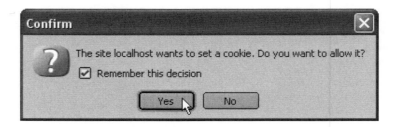

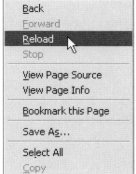

When the page first loads the value of the **count** variable has been incremented from zero to a value of one. The name and value of this variable are stored in the associated file in the temporary directory on the server. Each time the page is reloaded the value is retrieved from that file, incremented and the new value is stored.

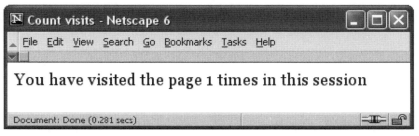

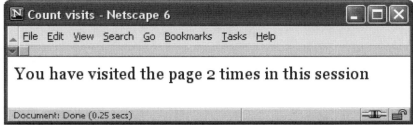

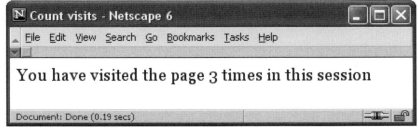

Open the file in the server's temporary directory in a text editor to see how the session variable name and value are stored.

Sessions without cookies

The example on the previous page demonstrated how the **PHPSESSID** cookie is used to store the unique identifier required by the session process. This would seem to duplicate the ability to store and retrieve data directly in cookies.

There is, however, another way to make the unique identifier accessible across an entire website without requiring the browser to accept cookies. This method appends the unique identifier to the URL in each hyperlink to other pages on that website.

This method is more reliable than using cookies as some users prefer to set their browsers to decline cookies, so the intended functionality of the PHP script will not work.

When the unique identifier is found in a **PHPSESSID** cookie the **SID** constant is then set to null.

PHP has a constant called **SID** that contains details of the unique session identifier as a **key-value** pair. Here **PHPSESSID** is the **key** and the identifier string is the **value**. This can be simply added to the URL in a hyperlink as a query string. The syntax to do this uses the URL, followed by a question mark, followed by **SID**, such as:

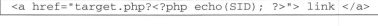

```
<a href="target.php?<?php echo(SID); ?>"> link </a>
```

To disable cookies in Netscape/ Mozilla browsers navigate through **Edit-Preferences-Privacy & Security-Cookies** then click the radio button option to **Disable cookies.**

When the link is followed the session identifier is sent to the target page, thus making the session variables available on that page.

The following example is illustrated using a Netscape browser with cookies disabled running on Windows. For testing, it is easier to disable cookies in Netscape than it is in Internet Explorer. The first page starts the session and provides a hyperlink to another page with the **SID** appended as a query string. Both pages display the contents of the **SID** constant to reveal the unique identifier.

session_start.php

```
<?php session_start(); ?>

<html><head><title>Session starter</title><head> <body>

<a href="next.php?<?php echo(SID); ?>">Next page</a>

<hr>

<? echo(SID); ?>

</body></html>
```

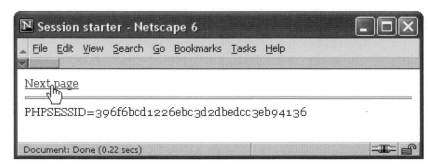

Because the link on the second page returns to the page that started the session it does not need to send the session ID. Links to other pages would need to send the session ID to make session variables available to them.

The target page of the link first uses the **session_is_registered()** function to see if a session variable called **count** already exists. If not found, it will be created by the **session_register()** function. The current count value is then incremented. A link is included to return to the first page then the current **count** value is displayed along with the **SID** constant contents.

next.php

```
<?php       if ( !session_is_registered("count") )
            { session_register("count"); }
            $count++;
?>
<html><head><title>Session running</title><head> <body>
<a href="session_start.php">Go to previous page</a> <hr>

<?php echo("You have been here $count times"); ?>
<br> <br>
<?php echo(SID); ?>

</body></html>
```

Repeatedly following the links back and forth, or reloading the second page, reveals successively higher count values.

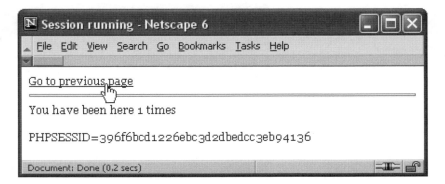

Setting session preferences

This example demonstrates how to access a users chosen preference across multiple pages using a session variable called **session_font**. The session ID is passed with the URL links by appending the PHP **SID** constant so that the user's preference can be accessed from any page – even if cookies are disabled.

prefs1.php

```php
<?php     session_start();

    if($font != null)
    {    if( ! session_is_registered("session_font") )
         { session_register("session_font"); }
         $session_font = $font;
         header("Location:prefs2.php?".SID);
         exit();
    }
?>
<html><head><title>Session preferences</title></head>
<body> <h3>Select Your Preferred Font Family</h3>
<form action="<?php echo($PHP_SELF); ?>" method="post">
<input type="radio" name="font" value="serif">Serif
<input type="radio" name="font" value="sans-serif">
Sans-Serif
<input type="radio" name="font" value="monospace">
Monospace
<input type="radio" name="font" value="cursive">Cursive
<input type="radio" name="font" value="fantasy">Fantasy
<br> <br> <input type="submit" value="Submit">
</form> </body></html>
```

*Notice that each of these three pages begins by calling the **session_start()** function to enable session variables to be used within each page.*

*When this form is submitted with one of the radio buttons selected the script registers a session variable called **session_font** then assigns the chosen button's value to it. The browser is then redirected.*

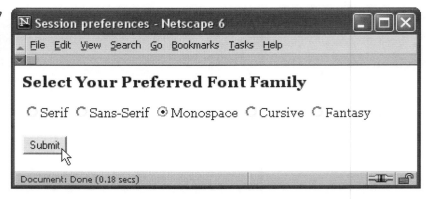

prefs2.php

```
<?php  session_start(); ?>
<html><head><title>Session running</title>
<style type="text/css">
  body { font-family:<?php echo($session_font); ?>; }
</style>
</head> <body><h3>Preferred font family is
<?php echo($session_font); ?></h3>
<a href="prefs3.php?<?php echo(SID); ?>">Next page</a>
</body></html>
```

*The second page in this example assigns the **session_font** variable's value in a style sheet — so that body content is displayed in the font family selected on the first page. The link to another page again appends the session ID **SID** constant.*

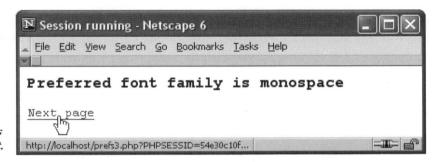

prefs3.php

```
<?php session_start(); ?>
<html><head><title>Session still running</title>
<style type="text/css">
  body { font-family:<?php echo($session_font); ?>; }
</style>
</head><body><h3>Preferred font family is still
<?php echo($session_font); ?> </h3>
<a href="prefs1.php?<?php echo(SID); ?>">
Change font?</a>     </body></html>
```

*The third page in this example again assigns **session_font** in a style sheet — so that body content is displayed in the font family selected on the first page. The link back to the first page allows selection of a different font family.*

Cookies or sessions?

Cookies are the optimal method for maintaining data with PHP and it is extremely simple to store the data with the **set_cookie()** function. Cookies are perhaps easier to use than sessions.

Unfortunately cookies require the co-operation of the user's browser in allowing cookies to be stored on the client system. As concerns about privacy and security become heightened, with increasing fear of computer viruses, more users than ever are becoming reluctant to allow cookies on their systems. This prevents you from using cookies to store data for PHP routines.

Some of the newly emerging mobile devices which can access the Internet may not even have the capacity to store cookies.

On the other hand, storing data in session variables does not rely upon the user's browser settings so is far more reliable than using cookies. You just have to remember to append the **SID** session identifier onto each URL in hyperlinks, and to call the **session_start()** function at the beginning of each page.

Changing the PHP configuration can even remove the need to call **session_start()** manually on each page. In the session block of the **phpinfo.php** page is a directive called **session.auto_start** that by default is set to **off** on installation.

Save the php.ini file after editing to apply the changes.

Open the **php.ini** file in a text editor and find the entry for **session.auto_start**. Change its value from **0** to **1** to turn this feature on. Now PHP will automatically perform the tasks of the **session_start()** function whenever a page gets loaded.

With **session.auto_start** set to **on**, each of the three calls to the **session_start()** function in the example on page 122/123 can be removed – and the preference data is still maintained as the user navigates between the pages.

Overall it may be better to use sessions rather than cookies, especially in PHP scripts that need to store critical data, such as selected shopping cart items on an e-commerce website.

Sessions ensure that stored data will be available across the entire website, even in those browsers where cookies are not enabled, but this will use more server resources to store the data.

Sending email with PHP

This chapter features a feedback form on a Web page where visitors can enter comments which will automatically be sent to a specified email address by PHP. Examples demonstrate how to send plain text messages, HTML-formatted messages and emails with attachments. Error-checking is added to prevent the submission of incomplete forms.

Covers

Enabling PHP email | 126

Creating a feedback form | 127

Sending plain text email | 128

Sending HTML email | 130

Creating an attachment form | 132

Sending attachments with email | 134

Adding error-checking | 136

Validating email address formats | 138

Chapter Ten

Enabling PHP email

PHP must be configured correctly in the **php.ini** file with the details of how your system sends email. Open **php.ini** in a text editor then find the section headed **[mail function]**.

Windows users should ensure that two directives are supplied. The first is called **SMTP** (Simple Mail Transfer Protocol) and defines your email server address. The second is called **sendmail_from** and defines your own email address.

The configuration for Windows should look something like this:

Installation may have automatically set the necessary directives but it is still worth checking them.

Linux users simply need to let PHP know the location of their **sendmail** application. The path, and any desired switches, should be specified to the **sendmail_path** directive.

The configuration for Linux should look something like this

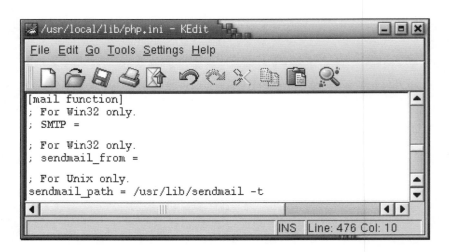

Creating a feedback form

The feedback form shown below is used to submit user data by email in the examples throughout this chapter. It is a HTML page containing a form with three input fields named **username**, **useraddr** and **comments**. When the form is submitted their values are sent to the form-handler **feedback.php** shown on the next page.

feedback.html

```html
<html>
  <head>
    <title>Feedback Form</title>
  </head>
  <body>
    <form action="feedback.php" method="post">
     Name:<input type="text" name="username" size="30"/>
     <br> <br>
     Email:<input type="text" name="useraddr" size="30">
     <br> <br>
     <textarea name="comments" cols="30" rows="5">
     </textarea><br/>
     <input type="submit" value="Send Form">
    </form>
  </body>
</html>
```

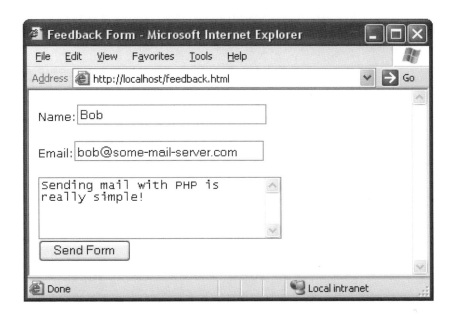

Sending plain text email

The PHP **mail()** function makes it easy to send email using scripts. This function requires three mandatory arguments that specify the recipient's email address, the subject of the message, then the actual message itself. So the **mail()** function syntax looks like this:

```
mail( to, subject, message );
```

As soon as the **mail()** function is called PHP will attempt to send the email then it will return **true** if successful, or **false** if it failed.

Multiple recipients can be specified as the first argument to the **mail()** function in a comma-separated list.

The example that follows is a form handler for the feedback form created on the previous page. It assigns the recipient's address and a subject title to two variables. The user's entry into the feedback form's **comment** textarea is assigned to a third variable. These variables are then specified as the three arguments to the **mail()** function when it is called to send the email message.

feedback.php

```php
<?php
    #recipient's email address
    $to = "php_ineasysteps@hotmail.com";

    #subject of the message
    $re = "Web Site Feedback";

    #message from the feedback form
    $msg = $comments;

    #send the email now...
    mail($to,$re,$msg);
?>

<html><head><title>Message Received</title></head>
<body>
<h3>Thanks for your comments</h3>

Message received from <?php echo($username); ?><br>

Reply to <?php echo($useraddr); ?>

</body></html>
```

The user's entries into the **username** and **useraddr** text fields of the feedback form are used to display a confirmation that the message has been received.

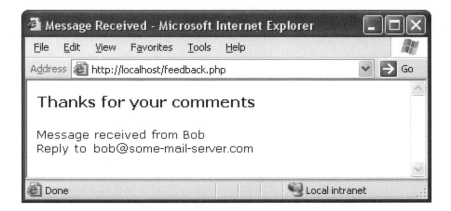

The email message is sent to the address specified as the first argument to the **mail()** function. Its subject is specified by the second argument. The actual message is specified by the third argument, as illustrated below:

*Notice that the sender of this message is that specified to the **send_from** directive in the **php.ini** file – not the user's email address.*

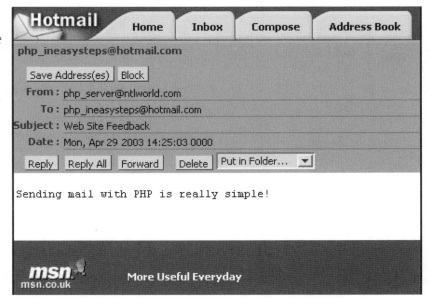

Sending HTML email

The PHP **mail()** function optionally accepts a fourth argument that can be used to specify a string of extra headers to be sent with all emails. Each header must be separated by **/r/n** – representing a carriage return and a newline.

The following example illustrates additions to the feedback form handler to allow HTML formatting by setting the **Content-type:** header to **text/html**.

*Note that the **Cc:** header is case-sensitive – **CC:** or **cc:** are incorrect.*

It then assigns the email address entered by the user, in the **useraddr** form field, to the **From:** header. Also the **Cc:** header is given another email address where a copy of each email should go.

All header information is contained in the **$headers** variable that is specified as the fourth argument to the **mail()** function.

When a form is submitted the header information and the message are sent, then a confirmation, like the one on page 129, is displayed.

feedback.php (modified)

*It is essential to set **MIME-Version: 1.0** in this example.*

```php
<?php    $to = "php_ineasysteps@hotmail.com";
         $re = "Web Site Feedback";
         $msg = $comments;

         #set the Content-type header for HTML mail
         $headers  = "MIME-Version: 1.0\r\n";
         $headers .= "Content-type: text/html; ";
         $headers .= "charset=iso-8859-1\r\n";

         #set the From: header
         $headers .= "From: $useraddr \r\n";

         #set the Cc: header
         $headers .= "Cc: another@hotmail.com \r\n";

         #send the email now...
         mail($to,$re,$msg, $headers);
?>
<html><head><title>Message Received</title></head>
<body> <h3>Thanks for your comments</h3>
Message received from <?php echo($username); ?><br>
Reply to <?php echo($useraddr); ?>
</body></html>
```

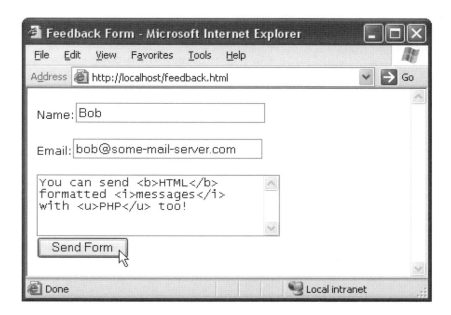

HTML formatting tags can now be included in the user's entry and are applied to the received message. When this form is submitted the user's comments are received in the format shown below:

*Notice that this email appears to be sent from the user's own email address and the Cc: has been added. The From: header has replaced the **send_from** directive value. Clicking on the **reply** button will now open a blank email form with the user's own address given as the recipient.*

Creating an attachment form

To send an attachment with an email message an **enctype** attribute must be added to the HTML <form> element and assigned a value of **multipart/form-data**.

This example builds on the previous feedback form by adding input fields for subject and file attachment. The user can push the **Browse** button to open a dialog box that lets them select a file to attach to the message. When this form is submitted the values entered in the fields named **to**, **from**, **re**, **comments** and **att** are sent to the form-handler **sendmixed.php**, that is listed on page 134.

sendmixed.html

This example puts the inputs inside table cells for better presentation.

```
<html><head><title>Attachment Form</title></head>
<body>
<form action="sendmixed.php" method="post"
                            enctype="multipart/form-data">
<table>
<tr><td>To:</td>
    <td><input type="text" name="to" size="40"/></td>
</tr>
<tr><td>From:</td>
    <td><input type="text" name="from" size="40" /></td>
</tr>
<tr><td>Subject:</td>
    <td><input type="text" name="re" size="40" /></td>
</tr>
<tr><td>Message:</td>
    <td>
    <textarea cols="30" rows="5" name="comments">
    </textarea>
    </td>
</tr>
<tr><td>Attachment:</td>
    <td><input type="file" name="att" size="26" /></td>
</tr><td colspan="2">
    <input type="submit" value="Send Form" />
    </td>
</tr>
</table>
</form>
</body></html>
```

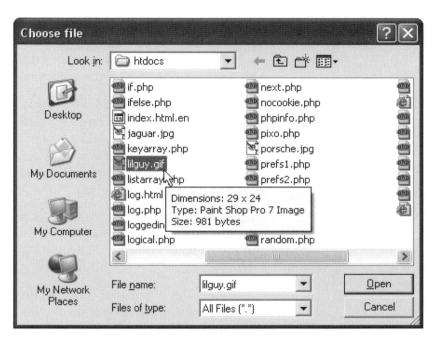

Sending attachments with email

To send an email with mixed content requires a more advanced understanding of email formats. A main **Content-Type:** header must first declare the content to be **multipart/mixed**. Then text and attachment sections can be specified within **boundaries**.

A **boundary** is started with two hyphens followed by a unique number which cannot appear in the message part of the email. It is common to use the PHP **md5()** function to create a 32 digit hexadecimal number for this purpose. The **time()** function can be specified as its argument to seed the number. A final **boundary** denoting the email's final section must also end with two hyphens.

*Remember that $att_name, $att_size and $att_type variables are automatically created for the HTML file input named **att** when the form is submitted – see page 106 for details.*

Attached files should be encoded with the **base64_encode()** function for safer transmission and are best split into chunks with the **chunk_split()** function. This adds **\r\n** inside the file at regular intervals, normally every 76 characters.

The following commented code lists the form handler for the attachment form that was created on the previous page:

sendmixed.php

*The boundary number is assigned to the **boundary** attribute in the main **Content-Type:** header.*

```php
<?php

    #variables passed are $to,$from,$re,$comments,$att

    #open the file
    $fp = fopen( $att_name, "r");

    #read the file into a variable
    $file = fread( $fp, $att_size );

    #encode the data for safe transit
    #and insert \r\n every 76-characters
    $file = chunk_split(base64_encode($file));

    #get a random 32-character hexadecimal number
    $num = md5( time() );

    #define the main headers
    $hdr  = "From:$from\r\n";
    $hdr .= "MIME-Version: 1.0\r\n";
    $hdr .= "Content-Type: multipart/mixed; ";
    $hdr .= "boundary=$num\r\n";
    $hdr .= "--$num\r\n";                    #start boundary here
```

sendmixed.php
(continued)

The **Content-Transfer-Encoding:** header for the text is plain **8bit**, which is its natural state. The attachment has been encoded with the **base64_encode()** function so is described as **base64**. The **Content-Disposition:** header is described here as **attachment** but could alternatively be **inline** to include the attachment in the email message body.

```php
    #define the message section
    $hdr .= "Content-Type: text/plain\r\n";
    $hdr .= "Content-Transfer-Encoding: 8bit\r\n\n";
    $hdr .= "$comments\r\n";
    $hdr .= "--$num\n";                    #start boundary here

    #define the attachment section
    $hdr .= "Content-Type: $att_type; ";
    $hdr .= "name=\"$att_name\"\r\n";
    $hdr .= "Content-Transfer-Encoding: base64\r\n";
    $hdr .= "Content-Disposition: attachment; ";
    $hdr .= "filename=\"$att_name\"\r\n\n";
    $hdr .= "$file\r\n";
    $hdr .= "--$num--";                    #final boundary here

    #send the email now...
    mail( $to, $re, "", $hdr);

    #close the file
    fclose($file);
?>
```

Notice how a pair of quotes are used in the **mail()** function arguments to skip the **message** argument.

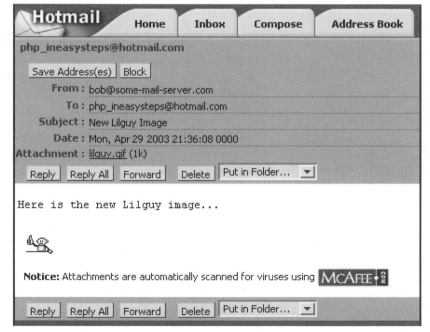

Adding error-checking

Previous examples in this chapter have created a form page and a separate form-handler page but this examples combines the feedback form from page 127 with the form-handler script on page 128 on a single page.

It assigns the **PHP_SELF** environment variable to the form's **action attribute** so that the page is reloaded when the form is submitted. The entire HTML form is contained inside a variable named **$form** which is written on the page when it is first loaded.

Assigning the $username, $useraddr and $comments variables to the input fields ensures that any entered values are retained when the form is submitted.

The script ensures that all input fields have been completed before it will send the email, otherwise it will write appropriate error messages then rewrite the form, complete with any entered values.

When all input fields have entries, the variable called **$valid** remains **true** so the email is sent and a confirmation is displayed.

```
<html><head><title>Combined Feedback Form</title></head>
<body>
<?php       #the HTML form that can be written dynamically
$form ="<form action=\"$PHP_SELF\" method=\"post\">";
$form.="Name:<input type=\"text\" name=\"username\"";
$form.=" size=\"30\" value=\"$username\" > <br> <br>";
$form.="Email:<input type=\"text\" name=\"useraddr\"";
$form.=" size=\"30\" value=\"$useraddr\"> <br> <br>";
$form.="Comments:<textarea name=\"comments\" ";
$form.="cols=\"30\" rows=\"5\">$comments</textarea>";
$form.="<br> <input type=\"submit\" name=\"sent\" ";
$form.="value=\"Send Form\"></form>";

#execute this code if the form has been submitted once
if($sent)
{ $valid=true;              #set variable default value

  #check username field is not blank
  if( !$username )
  { $errmsg.="Enter your name...<br>"; $valid = false; }

  #check email useraddr field is not blank
  if( !$useraddr )
  { $errmsg .="Enter your email address...<br>";
    $valid = false; }
```

if($sent) is equivalent to if($sent==true) and it will be null until the form is submitted. Similarly if(!$username) is equivalent to if($username !=null) and it will be null if the input is empty when the form is submitted.

combined.php
(continued)

```php
    #check comments field is not blank
    if( !$comments )
    { $errmsg.="Enter your comments...<br>";
      $valid = false;
    }
}

#if invalid write the error message/s and the form
if($valid!=true)
{ echo( $errmsg.$form ); }
else    #if the form is valid send the email
{       $to = "php_ineasysteps@hotmail.com";
        $re = "Feedback from $username";
        $msg = $comments;
        $headers = "From: $useraddr \r\n";

        if(mail($to,$re,$msg, $headers))
        { echo("Thanks for your comments, $username");}
}
?>
</body></html>
```

The **$errmsg**
variable stores
any error
messages . It is
concatenated
to the **$form** variable,
containing the entire HTML
form, then written on the
page when an incomplete
form has been submitted.

This illustration
shows the page
after the form
has been
submitted
without any entry in the
comments input field.

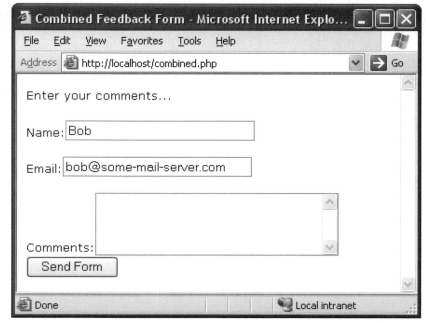

Validating email address formats

PHP's **preg_match()** function can assess if an email address appears to be in the expected format by matching permitted patterns for each part of the address.

The example on page 136 could be modified with the code below that checks for **@** and **.** symbols, and permitted characters.

(modified section for) combined.php

The **trim()** function removes any leading and trailing spaces.
See page 75 for more about **preg_match()**.

```php
if( !$useraddr )
{ $errmsg .="Enter your email address...<br>";
  $valid = false; }
else
{ $useraddr = trim($useraddr);
  #patterns for name,domain and top-level domains
  $_name = "/^[-!#$%&\'*+\\.\/0-9=?A-Z^_`{|}~]+";
  $_host = "([-0-9A-Z]+\.)+";
  $_tlds = "([0-9A-Z]){2,4}$/i";
  #check validity of email format
  if( !preg_match($_name."@".$_host .$_tlds,$useraddr) )
  {$errmsg.="Email address has incorrect format!<br>";
   $valid=false; }
}
```

This illustrates the page after the form has been submitted with an incomplete email address – no top-level domain part.

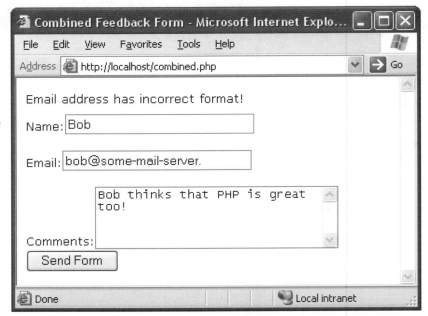

Getting started with MySQL

This chapter illustrates how to store information in a database. It demonstrates some basics of the Structured Query Language (SQL) that is used to add and manipulate data inside databases.

Covers

Introducing databases | 140

Exploring database tables | 141

Creating a new database | 142

Creating a database table | 143

SQL data types | 144

SQL field modifiers | 145

Inserting table data | 146

Altering an existing table | 147

Updating records | 148

Deleting data, tables & databases | 149

SQL queries | 150

Chapter Eleven

Introducing databases

Databases are simply convenient storage containers that store data in a structured manner. Every database is composed of one or more tables that structure the data into organized rows and columns. This makes it easier to reference and manipulate the data.

Each database table column has a label to identify the data stored within the table cells in that column. Each row contains an entry called a **record** that places data in each cell along that row.

A typical simple database table looks like this:

```
+-----------+-------+---------+----------+----------------+
| member_id | fname | lname   | tel      | email          |
+-----------+-------+---------+----------+----------------+
|         1 | John  | Smith   | 555-1234 | john@mail.com  |
|         2 | Anne  | Jones   | 555-5678 | anne@mail.com  |
|         3 | Mike  | McGrath | 555-3456 | mike@mail.com  |
+-----------+-------+---------+----------+----------------+
```

Column label **member_id** features an underscore character because spaces are not allowed in labels.

The rows of a database table are not automatically arranged in any particular order so they can be sorted alphabetically, numerically or by any other criteria. It is important, therefore, to have some means to identify each record in the table. The example above allocates a **member id** for this purpose and this unique identifier is known as the **primary key**.

Storing data in a single table is very useful but **relational** databases with multiple tables introduce more possibilities by allowing the stored data to be combined in a variety of ways. For instance, the following two tables could be added to the database containing the first example table shown above:

```
+----------+--------------+          +-----------+----------+
| video_id | title        |          | member_id | video_id |
+----------+--------------+          +-----------+----------+
|        1 | Titanic      |          |         2 |        1 |
|        2 | Men In Black |          |         1 |        3 |
|        3 | Star Wars    |          |         3 |        2 |
+----------+--------------+          +-----------+----------+
```

The table on the left lists several video titles sorted numerically by **video id** number. The table on the right describes a relationship between the tables that links each member to the video they have rented. So Anne (member #2) has Titanic (video #1), John (member #1) has Star Wars (video #3) and Mike (member #3) has Men In Black (video #2).

Exploring database tables

Open the MySQL monitor in a root shell window, or a Command Prompt window on Windows systems, then type **show databases;** at the **mysql>** prompt to see all the available databases.

For details on running the MySQL monitor Windows users should refer back to page 14, and Linux users should see page 21.

The MySQL installation creates two databases by default – one empty one called **test**, and one called **mysql** that is used by MySQL itself. The SQL command **use** *database-name;* selects a database to work with.

Type **use mysql;** to select the **mysql** database, then type the **show tables;** command to reveal a list of tables inside that database.

The SQL command **explain** *table-name;* can be used to see the format of a table. This displays all the field names in the table together with details of the data they may contain. Using the **mysql** database, type **explain user;** to see the format of the **user** table.

*The **explain** command does not reveal the actual data in the table, but merely the table format – see page 146 to discover how to view the table data.*

Creating a new database

MySQL databases can be created and their contents amended or queried in the MySQL monitor using Structured Query Language (SQL) commands.

The SQL command **create database** *database-name*; is used to create a new database.

Open the MySQL monitor then type **create database garage;** to create a new database called **garage**.

In Windows XP the MySQL server can be started, paused and stopped by the Management Console in Control Panel > Administrative Tools > Services.

The MySQL monitor responds by confirming that the new database has been created with the message **Query OK** followed by information about affected rows and time elapsed.

The names of all databases on the MySQL server can be viewed with the SQL **show databases;** command to confirm that the new **garage** database does indeed exist:

If a database with your chosen name already exists MySQL will not create a new database but will respond with this error message:

ERROR1007: Can't create database 'garage'. Database exists.

Creating a database table

To create a database table you must first select the database where it is to be added using the SQL **use** *database-name*; command. This requires the name of one of the existing databases, revealed by the **show databases;** command.

A semi-colon is required after each complete command.

A new table is created with the SQL **create table** *table-name*; command specifying a chosen name for that table, then a comma-separated list of chosen column names enclosed within a pair of brackets. Additionally each column name must be followed by a **data type** specifier to determine the type of data permitted in the table cells of that column. These specifiers can state the SQL keywords of **int** for integer numbers, **decimal** for floating-point numbers, or **text** for character strings.

For instance, the syntax to create a table with three columns is:
create table *table-name* **(***column1-name column1-type**,* *column2-name column2-type**,* *column3-name column3-type***)**;

Once a database has been selected the SQL **show tables;** command reveals the name of all tables in that database. This is used in the MySQL monitor illustrated below to confirm the addition of a table called **cars** to the **garage** database created on the facing page. The **cars** table contains one numeric column called **id**, and two text columns called **make** and **model**. Other SQL column types and further table creation options are described on the next page.

To close the MySQL monitor type "exit" or "quit" at the MySQL prompt.

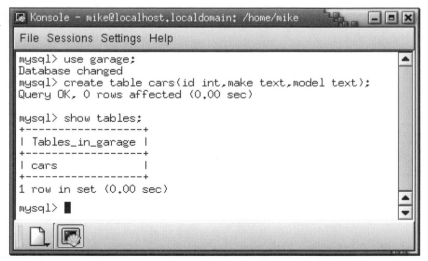

SQL data types

The table below describes the range of data type specifiers that can be used when creating table columns in MySQL. It is advisable to specify the permitted data type precisely. For instance, if a column is only going to hold short strings use **varchar()** rather than **text**.

Type	Description
int	An integer from -2147483648 to 2147483647
decimal	A floating point number that can specify the number of permissable digits. For example decimal(3,2) allows -999.99 to 999.99
double	A long double-precision floating point number
date	A date in theYYYY-MM-DD format
time	A time in the HH:MM:SS format
datetime	A combined date and time in the format YYYY-MM-DD HH:MM:SS
year	A year 1901-2155 in either YY or YYYY format
timestamp	Automatic date and time of last record entry
char()	A string of defined <u>fixed</u> length up to 255 characters long. For example, char(100) pads a smaller string to make it 100 characters long
varchar()	A string of defined <u>variable</u> length up to 255 characters long that is stored without padding
text	A string up to 65535 characters long
blob	A binary type for variable data
enum	A single string value from a defined list. For example, enum("red","green","blue") allows entry of any one of these three colors only
set	A string or multiple strings from a defined list. For example, set("red","green","blue") allows entry of one or more of these three colors

An enum type can contain up to 65535 permissible elements.

SQL field modifiers

In addition to specifying permissible data types when creating database table columns the modifiers described in the following table can optionally be stated to further control how a column should be used:

Modifier	Description
not null	Insists that each record must include data entry in this column
unique	Insists that records may not duplicate any entry in this column
auto_increment	Available only for numeric columns to automatically generate a number that is one more than the previous value in that column
primary key()	Specifies as its argument the name of the column to be used as the primary key for that table. For example, primary key(id)

*At the MySQL prompt type **explain cars;** to see how the table is defined.*

Modifiers could be included when creating the **cars** table on page 143 to produce a table with better defined columns. The **create table** *table-name*; command shown in the MySQL monitor below can automatically number the primary key **id** column. Each record must now include data in the **make** and **model** columns although no duplicate entries are permitted in the **model** column.

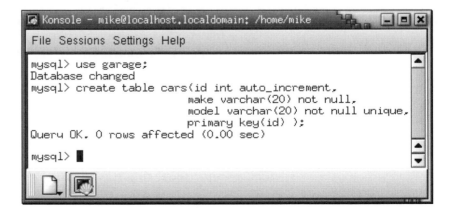

Inserting table data

Once a table has been created in a MySQL database data can be entered into it with the SQL **insert into** command.
The syntax to enter a complete record across a row is:
insert into *table-name* **values (***value1, value2, value3***);**

The data values are entered as comma-separated arguments to the SQL **values()** function and the list must correspond to the number of table columns and each value must be of the correct data type.

Enclose string data inside quotes when inserting data.

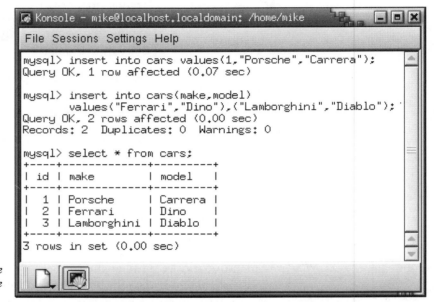

```
Konsole – mike@localhost.localdomain: /home/mike
File Sessions Settings Help

mysql> insert into cars values(1,"Porsche","Carrera");
Query OK, 1 row affected (0.07 sec)

mysql> insert into cars(make,model)
    values("Ferrari","Dino"),("Lamborghini","Diablo");
Query OK, 2 rows affected (0.00 sec)
Records: 2  Duplicates: 0  Warnings: 0

mysql> select * from cars;
+----+-------------+---------+
| id | make        | model   |
+----+-------------+---------+
|  1 | Porsche     | Carrera |
|  2 | Ferrari     | Dino    |
|  3 | Lamborghini | Diablo  |
+----+-------------+---------+
3 rows in set (0.00 sec)
```

*Notice that the **id** value for the second and third records has been generated automatically because of that column's **auto_increment** modifier.*

Another way to insert data into a table is to specify the column names where the data is to be added as a comma-separated list, such as **insert into** *table-name* **(***column-name, column-name***);**. The actual data to be inserted into the specified columns is then listed as the **values()** function arguments as usual.

SQL instructions in the illustration use both methods to add three records to the **cars** table created on the previous page.

An entire table can be viewed with a SQL **select ★ from** command, followed by the name of the table, and the obligatory semi-colon. The example above uses this command to view the **cars** table.

Altering an existing table

The definition of a column in an existing table can be altered using the SQL commands **alter table** and **modify**, with the following syntax:

alter table *table-name* **modify** *field-name type modifiers*;

New columns can be added to an existing table using the same **alter table** command but now with the SQL **add** keyword. The syntax to add an extra column looks like this:

alter table *table-name* **add** *field-name type modifiers*;

The example shown in the MySQL monitor below uses the **alter table** command to add a new extra column called **top_mph** to the **cars** table from the previous page. Data can now be entered into the new column using the SQL **update** command, that is demonstrated on the next page.

*The new top_mph column does not have a **not null** modifier so it is optional to enter data here.*

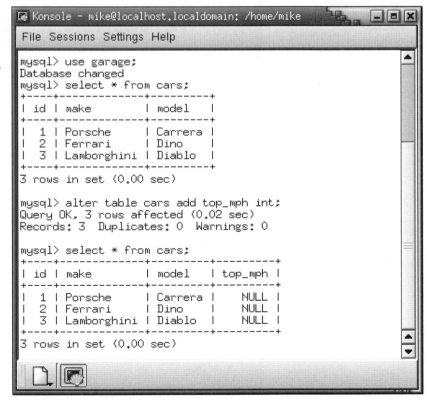

Updating records

All data values in an existing table column can be changed using the SQL **update** command with the SQL **set** keyword, like this:

update *table-name* **set** *field-name* = *new-value*;

More usefully, individual column values can be changed by adding a qualifier to this syntax with the SQL **where** keyword, like this:

update *table-name* **set** *field-name* = *new-value* **where** *id* = *int*;

This can be used in the **cars** table example from the previous page to update the **model** and **top_mph** columns, as shown below:

*Notice that **id** is used as the qualifier with these updates – except for the second and third instructions which use the value of the **make** column as their qualifier.*

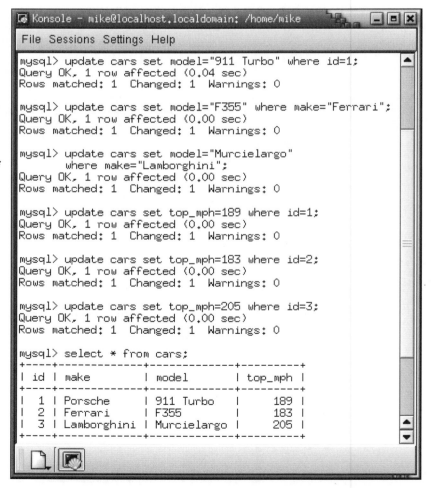

Deleting data, tables & databases

Records can be deleted from a table with the SQL **delete from** command followed by the table name. This needs to be used with some caution as the command **delete from cars;** would remove all the records from the **cars** table instantly.

Specific records can be deleted from a table by adding a **where** qualifier to the **delete from** command in order to identify a row. The command to delete the third record in the **cars** table is:

delete from cars where id=3;

Specific columns can be deleted from a table using the SQL **alter table** command followed by the table name, then the **drop** keyword followed by the column name. For instance, the command to delete the **top_mph** column from the **cars** table is:

alter table cars drop top_mph;

A complete table can be deleted from a database using the SQL **drop table** command followed by the table name. So the command to delete the **cars** table is:

drop table cars;

An entire database can be deleted with the SQL **drop database** command followed by the database name. The **garage** database that contained the **cars** table can be deleted with the command:

drop database garage;

This deletes the database and also destroys any tables contained within it so must obviously be used with care.

It is always a good idea to use the **show tables;** *command to check the contents before using **drop database.***

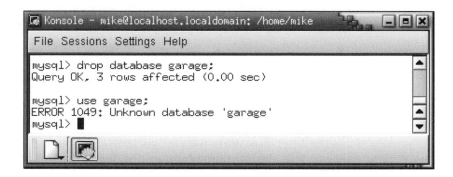

SQL queries

The basic SQL commands demonstrated in this chapter enable database tables to be created and filled with data. More advanced features of SQL allow the data to be queried for specific information. For instance, the **cars** table at the bottom of page 148 could be searched, to find the details of any car with a top speed exceeding 200 mph, with this query:

select * from cars where top_mph > 200;

In this case there is just one record that fits the bill:

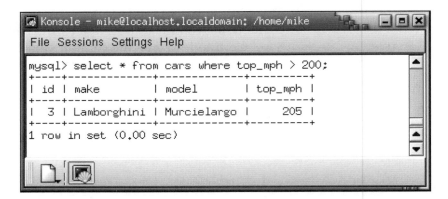

The ability to query data contained within databases is where the power of MySQL lies. More information illustrating the advanced features of the SQL language is given in the manual contained in the **Docs** folder of the MySQL installation directory.

Further details about SQL can also be found on the Internet in the MySQL Language Reference at **www.mysql.com**.

MySQL databases can be queried from PHP, using special functions which replicate the SQL commands used in this chapter.

Connecting to a MySQL database from PHP is made easy thanks to the PHP **mysql_connect()** function.

Once connected, the PHP **mysql_query()** function can be used to query the database and store the results in a PHP variable.

The next chapter demonstrates how to implement all the operations shown in this chapter from inside PHP scripts.

PHP & MySQL together

This chapter demonstrates how to create and manipulate MySQL databases from PHP scripts. The examples perform similar actions to the operations performed directly in the MySQL monitor in the previous chapter.

Covers

Creating a MySQL user & password | 152

Connecting a user to MySQL | 153

Listing databases | 154

Listing table names | 155

Creating a database | 156

Deleting a database | 157

Creating a database table | 158

Inserting table data | 161

Altering tables | 163

Retrieving data from a table | 164

More MySQL | 166

Chapter Twelve

Creating a MySQL user & password

The MySQL connection test made at the beginning of this book, right after installation, assumed connection to MySQL as the **root** user without any password. This affords poor security so in reality you should create a user with an associated password.

Adding a user is best achieved by entering a **grant statement** into the MySQL monitor as the **root** user. Opening the MySQL monitor as normal will commonly identify you as the **root** user. To be sure, from the MySQL monitor type **exit** to close the monitor. Then type this line to open the monitor as the **root** user:

mysql -u root

Or if a password has been set up for the root user the line will be:

mysql -u root -p *password*

Now at the mysql> prompt type this MySQL **grant statement**:

grant all privileges on *.* to *user-name@domain* **identified by** "*password*" **with grant option;**

This will create a new user with **superuser** status – allowing the named user full access from the specified domain, providing that they supply the specified password.

The illustration shows a new user (**mike**) being created in the **localhost** domain, with a simple password of **bingo** – these user details will often feature in future code examples in this book.

The commands are identical in Linux – but remember that you need a root shell window.

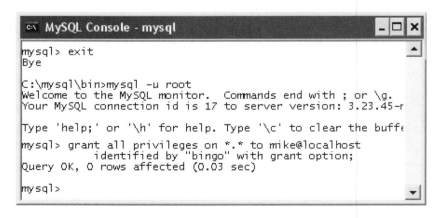

```
MySQL Console - mysql                                _ □ ✕

mysql> exit
Bye

C:\mysql\bin>mysql -u root
Welcome to the MySQL monitor.  Commands end with ; or \g.
Your MySQL connection id is 17 to server version: 3.23.45-r

Type 'help;' or '\h' for help. Type '\c' to clear the buffe

mysql> grant all privileges on *.* to mike@localhost
            identified by "bingo" with grant option;
Query OK, 0 rows affected (0.03 sec)

mysql>
```

Connecting a user to MySQL

To connect to MySQL the PHP **mysql_connect()** function requires three arguments specifying valid domain name, user name and password. This function returns **true** if the connection succeeds or **false** if the attempt fails. The script below writes a confirmation if the connection is successful.

connect.php

```php
<?php       $user = "mike";

$conn = mysql_connect( "localhost", $user, "bingo" );
if($conn){
$msg="Congratulations $user, You connected to MySQL"; }
?>
<html><head><title>Connecting user</title></head>
<body><h3> <?php echo($msg); ?> </h3></body></html>
```

Warning messages can be suppressed by preceding the function call with the @ symbol.

The user details are case-sensitive, so changing the value of the **$user** variable to **MIKE** produces these warning messages:

Listing databases

The equivalent of the SQL **show databases** command in PHP requires the use of three special functions.

Firstly, the **mysql_list_dbs()** function returns a **result set** of information about all databases and can be assigned to a variable.

The details of each database is held in separate rows inside the **result set** so the total number of databases can be determined using the **mysql_num_rows()** function to discover how many rows are in a **result set**. This function takes the **result set** as its argument.

The name of each database can be extracted from a **result set** by the **mysql_tablename()** function. This function is also used to extract the names of each table from a specified database. A **result set** and row number are required arguments to get the database names.

The example below assigns the **result set** to a variable called **$rs.** This is used as the argument to the **mysql_num_rows()** function to determine the length of a loop that lists each database name.

list-dbs.php

*Notice that this example uses the @ symbol to suppress warning messages and the **die()** function to write a message if the connection fails.*

```php
<?php
$conn = @mysql_connect("localhost","Mike","bingo")
        or die("Sorry - could not connect to MySQL");

$rs= mysql_list_dbs($conn);
for($row=0; $row < mysql_num_rows($rs); $row++)
{
   $db_list .= mysql_tablename($rs, $row)."<br>";
}
?>
<html><head><title>Listing databases</title></head>
<body><h3><?php echo($db_list); ?>   </h3></body></html>
```

Listing table names

Similar to the **mysql_list_dbs()** function, the PHP **mysql_list_tables()** function returns a **result set** of information about all tables in a database and this can be assigned to a variable.

Each table name can then be extracted by specifying the **result set**, and its row number in the **result set**, as the arguments to the **mysql_tablename() function**. The example below reveals the names of three tables that have been added to the **test** database.

list-tables.php

MySQL's own database (called **mysql**) must be excluded as its tables cannot be read in this way for security reasons.

```php
<?php $conn = @mysql_connect("localhost","mike","bingo")
        or die("Sorry - could not connect to MySQL");

$rs1= mysql_list_dbs($conn);
for($row=0; $row < mysql_num_rows($rs1); $row++)
{
   $this_db = mysql_tablename($rs1, $row);
   $list .= "<b>".$this_db."</b><br>";
   if($this_db != "mysql")
   {
     $rs2= mysql_list_tables($this_db);
     for($num=0; $num < mysql_num_rows($rs2); $num++)
     { $list.= " - ".mysql_tablename($rs2,$num)."<br>"; }
   }
}
?>

<html><head><title>Listing Tables</title></head>
<body> <?php  echo($list); ?> </body></html>
```

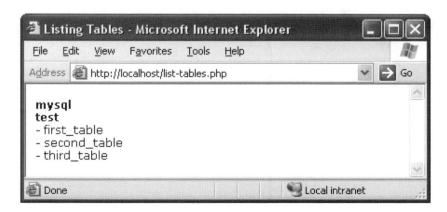

Creating a database

The PHP **mysql_create_db()** function attempts to create a database with the name supplied as its argument. The example below displays all existing databases then provides a form where a new database name can be input. When the form is submitted the script attempts to create a new database with the specified name.

create_db.php

*This function returns **true** if the database is successfully created or **false** if the attempt fails.*

```php
<?php
$conn = @mysql_connect("localhost","mike","bingo")
or die("Sorry - could not connect to MySQL");

$rs1=      @mysql_create_db( $db );

$rs2=      @mysql_list_dbs($conn);
for($row=0; $row < mysql_num_rows($rs2); $row++)
{ $list .= mysql_tablename($rs2, $row)." | "; }
?>
<html><head><title>Creating databases</title></head>
<body>
<form action="<?php echo($PHP_SELF); ?>" method="post">
Current databases: <?php echo($list); ?> <hr>
Name:<input type="text" name="db">
<input type="submit" value="Create database">
</form></body></html>
```

Deleting a database

The PHP **mysql_drop_db()** function attempts to delete a database with the name supplied as its argument. The example below mirrors that on the facing page but attempts to delete the specified database when the form is submitted. The function returns **true** if the attempt succeeds, or **false** if it fails.

delete_db.php

Notice how the @ symbol is used to suppress warnings.

```php
<?php
$conn = @mysql_connect("localhost","mike","bingo")
or die("Sorry - could not connect to MySQL");

$rs1=      @mysql_drop_db( $db );

$rs2=      @mysql_list_dbs($conn);
for($row=0; $row < mysql_num_rows($rs2); $row++)
{ $list .= mysql_tablename($rs2, $row)." | "; }
?>
<html><head><title>Deleting databases</title></head>
<body>
<form action="<?php echo($PHP_SELF); ?>" method="post">
Current databases: <?php echo($list); ?> <hr>
Name:<input type="text" name="db">
<input type="submit" value="Delete database">
</form></body></html>
```

Creating a database table

Once a database exists it can be selected for use with the PHP **mysql_select_db()** function that emulates the **use database;** SQL command. This function requires the database name and connection link as its two arguments.

An SQL command specified in PHP does not need the semi-colon terminator that is required when entering SQL commands directly in the MySQL monitor.

When a database has been selected operations can be performed on it by specifying SQL commands as arguments to the PHP **mysql_query()** function. So **create table** *table-name* can be used to create a new table inside a database.

This example creates an interface to dynamically create a new database table. It begins by seeking two variables. Initially these are not set so a form is written asking how many columns are required in the new table. When the form is submitted the script generates a different form with inputs for the names and data types of each field. When this completed form is submitted the value entered into each field is used to produce a SQL command that creates a database table with the chosen number of fields.

create_table.php

*When this first form is submitted with an entry in the input field the **$fields** variable is found to be set so the script moves onto the next section.*

```php
<html> <head> <title>Creating a table</title> </head>
<body>
<?php
if( !$fields and !$db )
{
 $form ="<form action=\"$PHP_SELF\" method=\"post\">";
 $form.="How many fields are needed in the new table?";
 $form.="<br><input type=\"text\" name=\"fields\">";
 $form.="<input type=\"submit\" value=\"Submit\">";
 echo($form);
}
```

The second form allows you to enter the name of an existing database to use, a name for the new table, column names with permissible data types and, optionally, field sizes.

create_table.php (continued)

In actuality the drop-down selection box is expanded to include options for all possible field data types – see page 144.

```php
else if( !$db )
{
  $form ="<form action=\"$PHP_SELF\" method=\"post\">";
  $form.="Database:
                <input type=\"text\" name=\"db\"><br>";
  $form.="Table Name:
                <input type=\"text\" name=\"table\"><br>";

for ($i = 0 ; $i <$fields; $i++) { $form.=
  "Column Name:<input type=\"text\" name=\"name[$i]\">";
$form.="Type: <select name=\"type[$i]\">";
$form.="<option value=\"char\">char</option>";
$form.="<option value=\"int\">int</option>";
#...plus options for all other possible data types...
$form.="</select> ";
$form.="Size:<input type=\"text\" name=\"size[$i]\">"; }

$form.="<input type=\"submit\" value=\"Submit\">";
$form.="</form>"; echo($form);
}
```

This form generates the appropriate number of field inputs from the value entered in the first form. When this completed form is submitted the $db variable is found to be set so the process moves on to the concluding section of the script, that is listed on the next page.

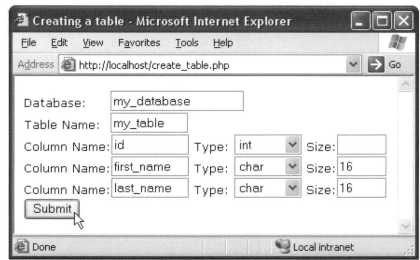

create_table.php
(continued)

```
else
{ #make the connection to mysql
 $conn = @mysql_connect("localhost", "mike", "bingo")
               or die("Err:Conn");
 #select the specified database
 $rs = @mysql_select_db($db, $conn) or die("Err:Db");
 #create the query
 $sql = "create table $table (";
 for ($i = 0; $i < count($name); $i++)
 { #field name & data type
   $sql .= "$name[$i] $type[$i]";
   #allow size specification for char and varchar types
   if(($type[$i] =="char") or ($type[$i] =="varchar"))
   { #if a size has been specified add it to the query
     if($size[$i] !="" ){ $sql.= "($size[$i])"; }
   }
   #if this is not the final field add a comma
   if(($i+1) != count($name) ){ $sql.=","; }
 } $sql .= ")";
 #display the SQL query
 echo("SQL COMMAND: $sql <hr>");
 #execute the query - attempt to create the table
 $result = mysql_query($sql,$conn) or die("Err:Query");
 #confirm if successful
 if ($result)
 { echo("RESULT: table \"$table\" has been created"); }
}
?> </body> </html>
```

This is the real business section of the script – it connects to MySQL, selects the specified database, builds an SQL query from the data entered in the previous form, then executes the query. The complete SQL command is displayed for reference and a confirmation is written.

You can also now see this new table in the MySQL console.

Creating a table - Microsoft Internet Explorer

File Edit View Favorites Tools Help

Address http://localhost/create_table.php

SQL COMMAND: create table my_table (id int,first_name char(16),last_name char(16))

RESULT: table "my_table" has been created

Done   Local intranet

Inserting table data

Adding record data to a database table employs the same technique that was used to create a new table in the previous example. The table is selected with the **mysql_select()** function, then an SQL query containing the record data is supplied as the argument to the **mysql_query()** function. This uses the SQL command **insert into** *table-name* followed by each piece of field data.

This example allows data to be entered into the **my_table** table that was created in the previous example:

add_record.php

In the list of SQL query values any string data should be surrounded by escaped quotes, as shown here.

The execution of this script is illustrated on the next page.

```
<html><head><title>Add record to my_database/my_table
</title></head><body>

<form action="<?php echo($PHP_SELF); ?>" method="post">
ID: <input type="text" name="id" size="3">
First Name: <input type="text" name="fname" size="8">
Last Name: <input type="text" name="lname" size="8"><br>
<input type="submit" value="Submit">
</form>

<?php
#ensure all fields have entries
if( $id and $fname and $lname)
{

   #connect to mysql
   $conn=@mysql_connect("localhost", "mike", "bingo")
                                  or die("Err:Conn");
   #select the specified database
   $rs = @mysql_select_db("my_database", $conn)
                                  or die("Err:Db");
   #create the query
   $sql="insert into my_table (id, first_name, last_name)
         values ( $id, \"$fname\", \"$lname\" )";

   #execute the query
   $rs=mysql_query($sql,$conn);

   #confirm the added record details
   if($rs){ echo("Record added:$id $fname $lname"); }
}
?>
</body></html>
```

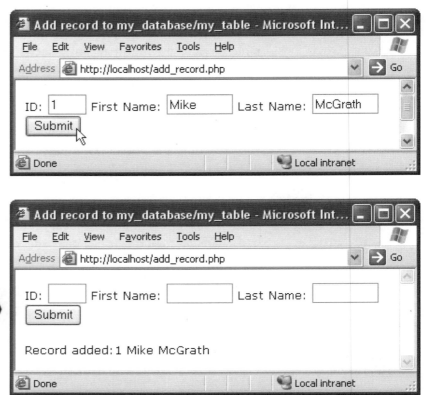

When the form is submitted a confirmation is written showing record details that were entered into the table. The illustration below shows the table in the MySQL console, using the SQL **select * from** *table-name*; command after adding more records.

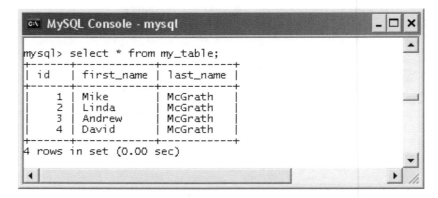

Altering tables

The table shown opposite does not specify the primary key field, disallow empty fields or duplicate entries. This can be improved by adding some of the field modifiers listed on page 145 with the SQL **alter table** *table-name* **modify** command.

The script below alters the **my_table** table on the facing page to make the **id** column automatically increment its values. Also the other two columns may not be left blank after adding the **not null** modifier and the first_name column may only accept **unique** data.

alter_table.php

The **alter** statements must include the columns' data types or the column specifications will not be modified.

```php
<?php #connect to MySQL
$conn=@mysql_connect("localhost", "mike", "bingo")
                or die("Err:Conn");

#select the specified database
$rs = @mysql_select_db("my_database", $conn)
                or die("Err:Db");

#create then execute the 1st query
$sql=
"alter table my_table modify id int auto_increment";
$rs=mysql_query($sql,$conn);

#create then execute the 2nd and 3rd queries
$sql="alter table my_table modify first_name char(16)
not null unique";
$rs=mysql_query($sql,$conn);
$sql="alter table my_table modify last_name char(16) not
null";
$rs=mysql_query($sql,$conn);
?>
```

Check the new table format in the MySQL monitor to see that the modifications have been applied.

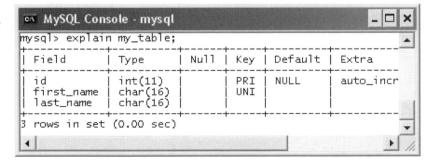

```
mysql> explain my_table;
+------------+----------+------+-----+---------+-----------+
| Field      | Type     | Null | Key | Default | Extra     |
+------------+----------+------+-----+---------+-----------+
| id         | int(11)  |      | PRI | NULL    | auto_incr |
| first_name | char(16) |      | UNI |         |           |
| last_name  | char(16) |      |     |         |           |
+------------+----------+------+-----+---------+-----------+
3 rows in set (0.00 sec)
```

Retrieving data from a database table

Data can be retrieved from a MySQL database using the SQL **select** *field-names* **from** *table-name* command to specify the fields required and the name of the table to search.

The PHP **mysql_fetch_array()** function returns an associative array of all the requested data from the table, row by row. This function requires the query **result set** as its argument. Each piece of data in the array is associated to the column name. The data is best assigned to an array variable using a **while** loop so that the data on each row can be retrieved using its associated column name on each iteration.

The following example retrieves the data from two columns of the **my_table** table , created on page 162. Each iteration of the loop assigns a row's data to an array called **$row** then the value associated with the column name on each row is written out.

get_data.php

```
<html><head><title>Get data</title></head>
<body>
<?php
#connect to MySQL
$conn=@mysql_connect("localhost", "mike", "bingo")
              or die("Err:Conn");

#select the specified database
$rs = @mysql_select_db("my_database", $conn)
              or die("Err:Db");

#create the query
$sql="select id,first_name from my_table";

#execute the query
$rs=mysql_query($sql,$conn);

#write the data
while( $row = mysql_fetch_array($rs) )
{
   echo("ID: ".$row["id"]);
   echo(" - FIRST NAME: ".$row["first_name"]."<br>");
}
?>
</body></html>
```

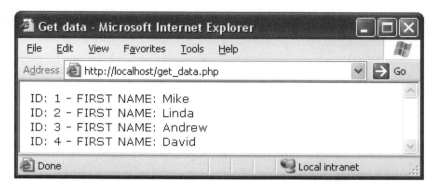

SQL queries that work in the MySQL monitor can be used as the first argument to the PHP mysql_query() function.

Data order can be specified by adding an **order by** clause to the end of the SQL query. Adding **order by first_name** to the end of the query opposite arranges the data alphabetically by **first_name**:

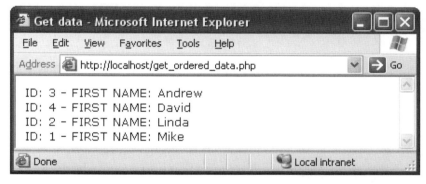

The method of working with MySQL via PHP follows this pattern –
1) connect to MySQL
2) select a database to use
3) build an SQL query
4) execute the query
5) now make use of the returned result set data.

Specific data can be retrieved by adding a **where** qualifier to the SQL query. For instance, adding **where id=3** to the query in the code shown opposite retrieves only data from that row:

More MySQL

The range of common basic database operations demonstrated in this chapter use just some of the features of MySQL. To discover ways to make MySQL even more flexible it is recommended that you download the MySQL manual.

The manual is available from the MySQL Web site at **http://mysql.com/documentation**, or one of its mirror sites.

As testimony to the widespread popularity of MySQL the manual is available in many languages, and in a variety of formats including HTML, Windows HLP format, PostScript, TexInfo and PDF.

A tutorial is included in the manual together with examples illustrating common database queries but, of course, these only give SQL code and do not feature any PHP scripts.

The MySQL Web site at **http://mysql.com** gives the latest news on the development of MySQL and posts details about forthcoming developers' conferences. It also offers a number of interesting User Stories where you can read how other people are using MySQL.

If you would prefer to work with MySQL via a Graphical User Interface (GUI), rather than from a command line, try the **MySQLGUI** program available at **http://mysql.com/downloads**. There are versions for both Windows and Linux.

DevShed Forums

Help with MySQL is available from the MySQL forum on the Developer Shed Web site at **http://forums.devshed**. It is worthwhile reading through past questions and answers to get a flavor of the forum before posting any questions yourself – and you may find the answer to your question is already there.

The main Developer Shed Web site at **www.devshed.com** is a great resource for learning more about MySQL as it features lots of articles submitted by developers. Many of these are in the form of a tutorial or discussion and often relate the story of a problem they have overcome using both MySQL and PHP together.

User authentication

This chapter demonstrates how to create a PHP log-in routine. The user name and password entered on the log-in page are authenticated against a list of valid user names and passwords which are stored in a MySQL database.

Covers

Creating a user table | 168

Adding authorized users | 170

Displaying authorized users | 172

The user log-in form | 174

The log-in form-handler script | 175

An authenticated log-in attempt | 176

Chapter Thirteen

Creating a user table

It is useful to restrict access to parts of a website by requiring visitors to enter a user name and password for authentication against a list of authorized users. A PHP script could verify the input against a list stored in a text file but it is faster and more efficient to maintain the list in a database table.

In this case the table will need to have four columns to store the user's first name, last name, user name and password. The table can be created using the **create_table.php** script described in the previous chapter on page 158–160.

First specify that four fields are needed, then submit the form.

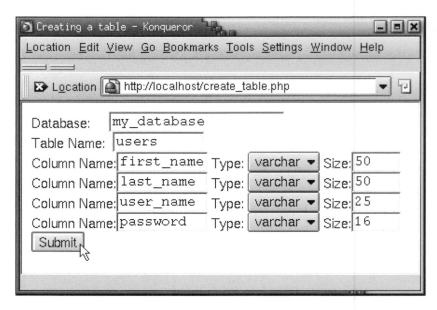

Next enter the name of the database to use and specify the new table name as **users**. Type the four field names **first_name**, **last_name**, **user_name** and **password** into the input fields and change each data type to **varchar**. Set the field lengths to 50 for the real names and just 25 for the user name. Allow a length of 16 for the password field because MySQL will store password information in encrypted form as a 16-digit hexadecimal number.

Now submit the form to create the new **users** table.

*When the completed form is submitted the SQL query creates the new table and the page displays a confirmation. The new **users** table can be viewed in the MySQL monitor to confirm its format.*

To ensure that all user names are unique alter the table to modify the user_name column – as shown in this illustration.

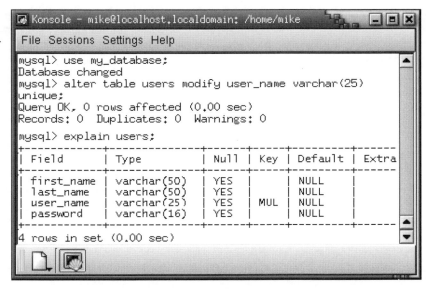

Adding authorized users

A form can be used to add details of each new user to the **user** database table that was created on the previous page. Each of four text inputs correspond to the table's four fields and are named **firstname**, **lastname**, **username** and **password**.

When the page is first loaded an **if-else** statement in the PHP script tests to see if values exist for each of these text inputs. If not, the script dynamically writes a form where their values can be entered.

The section of the script containing the form is listed below:

add_user.php

```
<html><head><title>Adding a User</title></head>
<body>
<?php
if( (!$firstname) or (!$lastname)
                    or (!$username) or (!$password) )
{
 $form ="Please enter all new user details...";
 $form.="<form action=\"$PHP_SELF\"";
 $form.=" method=\"post\">First Name: ";
 $form.="<input type=\"text\" name=\"firstname\"";
 $form.=" value=\"$firstname\"><br>Last Name: ";
 $form.="<input type=\"text\" name=\"lastname\"";
 $form.=" value=\"$lastname\"><br>User Name: ";
 $form.="<input type=\"text\" name=\"username\"";
 $form.=" value=\"$username\"><br>Password: ";
 $form.="<input type=\"text\" name=\"password\"";
 $form.=" value=\"$password\"><br>";
 $form.="<input type=\"submit\" value=\"Submit\">";
 $form.="</form>";
 echo($form);
}
```

*The PHP variables are assigned to the **value** attributes of each input so that if an incomplete form is submitted any text input that was completed will retain its original entry.*

When the fully completed form is submitted the **if** test finds that each of the inputs have entries so the script moves on to the **else** block. This connects to MySQL and selects the **user** table, then inserts each of the text input values into the appropriate column. If the new user is added successfully a confirmation is written.

The section of the script that adds the user's details to the database table is listed on the opposite page.

add_user.php
(continued)

```
else
{ $conn = @mysql_connect("localhost","mike","bingo")
    or die("Could not connect to MySQL"); #connect MySQL
  $db = @mysql_select_db("my_database",$conn)
    or die("Could not select database"); #select database
  $sql = "insert into users
    (first_name,last_name,user_name,password) values
    (\"$firstname\",\"$lastname\",\"$username\",
            password(\"$password\") )"; #create the query
  $result = @mysql_query($sql,$conn)
    or die("Could not execute query"); #execute the query
  if($result) { echo("New user $username added"); }
}
?> </body></html>
```

*The **password()** function used here is not PHP – it's a MySQL function that encrypts the password as a 16-digit hexadecimal number.*

Remember to surround the form variables with escaped quotes inside the SQL query.

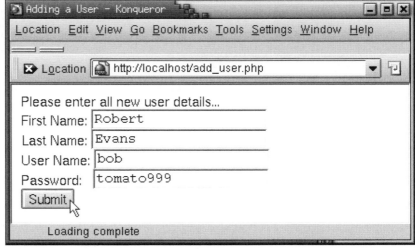

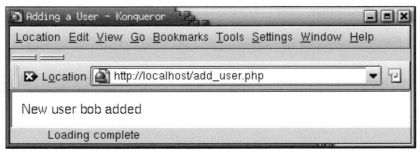

Displaying authorized users

The **add_user.php** interface from the previous page has been used to add a total of ten users to the **users** database table that was created at the beginning of this chapter.

Complete details of each user can be retrieved from the **users** database table and displayed in a HTML table format.

This script uses the SQL **select * from** *table-name* command to collect the entire data from the **users** database table.

A variable called **$list** is used to build a string containing a complete HTML table. This starts with a row of column headings for First Name, Last Name, User Name and Password. Each row of the **users** database table is then added to the string as a row in the HTML table. Once the HTML table is complete it is written out on the page to display all the users details.

get_users.php

```
<html><head><title>Get Users</title></head>
<body>

<?php

#connect to MySQL
$conn=@mysql_connect("localhost", "mike", "bingo")
        or die("Could not connect");

#select the specified database
$rs = @mysql_select_db("my_database", $conn)
        or die("Could not select database");

#create the SQL query
$sql="select * from users";

#execute the query
$rs=mysql_query($sql,$conn)
        or die("Could not execute query");;

#start building a HTML table for the users details
$list = "<table border=\"1\" cellpadding=\"2\">";
$list.="<tr><th>First Name</th>";
$list.="<th>Last Name</th>";
$list.="<th>User Name</th>";
$list.="<th>Password</th></tr>";
```

get_users.php
(continued)

```php
#loop through each row of the users database table
while($row= mysql_fetch_array($rs) )
{
  $list .= "<tr>";
  $list .= "<td>".$row["first_name"]."</td>";
  $list .= "<td>".$row["last_name"]."</td>";
  $list .= "<td>".$row["user_name"]."</td>";
  $list .= "<td>".$row["password"]."</td>";
  $list .= "</tr>";
}
$list .= "</table>";

#write out the list of users
echo($list);

?>
</body></html>
```

*Notice that the passwords are reproduced in the 16-digit hexadecimal format created by the MySQL **password()** function.*

Get Users – Konqueror

Location Edit View Go Bookmarks Tools Settings Window Help

Location http://localhost/get_users.php

First Name	Last Name	User Name	Password
Robert	Evans	bob	6a8d554d1f478f65
John	Smith	smiffy	104250a46cfe2db2
Sandra	Rhodes	sandy	36619db83843920e
Ann	Sanderson	annie	2a4d23e858edb385
Tom	Barring	tommy	6e4c16330be342f6
Mark	Preston	mark	390aea22779ec223
Geoff	Clark	clarky	2c803f906b2168a8
Gary	Truman	gaz	7493270443859433
Barbara	Melling	barbie	32d4840f006059ee
Maureen	Harris	mo	568979d613317e45

Loading complete

The user log-in form

A typical log-in page asks that the user's name and password should be entered into form text inputs. When the form is submitted these values can be checked against a table of authorized users by PHP.

The simple HTML page listed below names the input fields as **username** and **password** so their values will be sent to the PHP script opposite in variables named **$username** and **$password**.

authenticate.html

*The form's **action** attribute is assigned the name of the script on the opposite page to be its form-handler.*

```
<html><head><title>Log-In Page</title></head>
<body>
Please enter your user details to log-in here...

<form action="authenticate.php" method="post">
Username:<br>
<input type="text" name="username">
<br><br>
Password:<br>
<input type="text" name="password">
<br><br>
<input type="submit" value="Log In">
</form>

</body></html>
```

The log-in form-handler script

The form-handler script for the log-in form opposite first checks that there are entries in both **username** and **password** fields. If so the script looks in the **users** database table, created earlier in this chapter, and seeks matches to the **$username** and **$password** values. The number of table rows that do match is stored in a variable called **$num**. An **if-else** statement block then tests to see that at least one row matched and will either create a confirmation message or return the browser to the log-in page, depending on the result. If the log-in succeeds a welcome message is written out.

authenticate.php

Notice how the HTTP_REFERER environment variable is used to specify the address of the log-in page.

A successful log-in attempt is illustrated on the next page.

```php
<?php
#if either form field is empty return to the log-in page
if( (!$username) or (!password) )
{ header("Location:$HTTP_REFERER"); exit(); }

#connect to MySQL
$conn=@mysql_connect("localhost", "mike", "bingo")
    or die("Could not connect");

#select the specified database
$rs = @mysql_select_db("my_database", $conn)
    or die("Could not select database");

#create the SQL query
$sql="select * from users where user_name=\"$username\"
    and password = password( \"$password\" )";

#execute the query
$rs=mysql_query($sql,$conn)
    or die("Could not execute query");

#get number of rows that match username and password
$num = mysql_numrows($rs);

#if there is a match the log-in is authenticated
if($num != 0)
{ $msg = "Welcome $username - your log-in succeeded!"; }
else #or return to the log-in page
{ header("Location:$HTTP_REFERER"); exit(); }
?>

<html> <head><title>Log-In Authenticated</title></head>
<body> <?php echo($msg); ?> </body> </html>
```

An authenticated log-in attempt

The log-in page illustrated below shows user entries in the form text fields of **authenticate.html** that is listed on page 174. The **username** matches that of the user named Robert Evans in the first row of the **users** database table, shown on page 173.

When encrypted by the MySQL **password()** function the value in the **password** field will also match that of the user named Robert Evans. The form-handler script, **authenticate.php** – listed on the previous page, will find a match for these values on one row of the **users** database table so this log-in attempt will succeed.

A PHP guestbook

This chapter demonstrates a popular application of PHP as a guestbook for a website where visitors can leave comments. These are stored in a MySQL database and can be retrieved at any time for viewing in chronological order on a single page.

Covers

Creating a guestbook database table | 178

Signing the guestbook | 180

Inserting guestbook entries | 182

Using timestamp data | 183

Viewing the guestbook | 184

More PHP resources | 186

Chapter Fourteen

Creating a guestbook database table

A guestbook application first requires a database table be created to store the messages that visitors will leave. This can be achieved directly in the MySQL monitor, or with a PHP script.

The following script uses an existing database called **my_database**. There it creates a table called **guestbook** with fields for **id**, **name**, **email** address, **comments** and an automatic **timestamp** entry of the date and time that the message was recorded.

This script needs to be run just once to build the **guestbook** table.

guestbook-create.php

The 14–digit timestamp represents year(4), month(2), day number(2), hours(2), minutes(2) and seconds(2) – and in that order. For more details see page 183.

```html
<html>
<head> <title>Create guestbook table</title> </head>
<body>

<?php

  #connect to MySQL
  $conn = @mysql_connect("localhost","mike","bingo")
            or die("Could not connect to database");

  #select the database
  $rs = @mysql_select_db("my_database", $conn)
            or die("Could not select database");

  #create the SQL query
  $query = "id int(4) auto_increment,";
  $query.= "name varchar(50),";
  $query.= "email varchar(50),";
  $query.= "comments text,";
  $query.= "time timestamp(14), primary key(id)";

  $sql = "create table guestbook( $query )";

  #execute the query
  $rs = @mysql_query ($sql)
    or die("<h3>Could not create guestbook table <br>
                        Does it already exist?</h3>");

  #confirm the result
  echo("<h3>Created guestbook table</h3>");
?>
</body> </html>
```

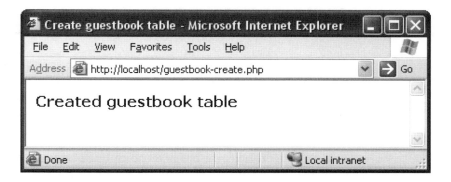

*You can confirm the format of the **guestbook** table in the MySQL monitor with the **explain table-name;** SQL command.*

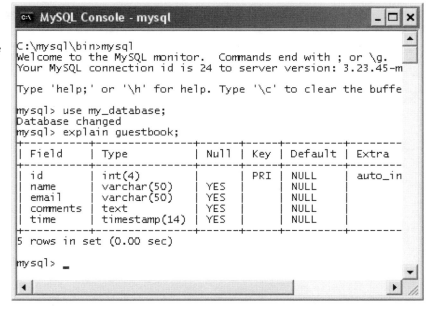

*Subsequent attempts to run this script will fail after the **guestbook** table has been created.*

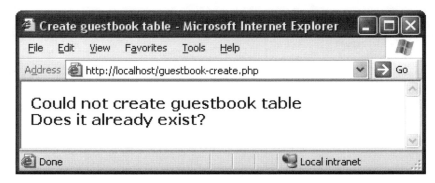

Signing the guestbook

Once the **guestbook** database table has been created, by the script on the previous page, data can be stored in it by submission from a HTML form using PHP.

When first loaded in a browser the following PHP script displays a form containing fields for **name**, **email** and **comments**. Upon submission the form will be displayed once more unless all three fields are not blank.

If the form has been completed correctly the script will add the input entries to the corresponding columns of the **guestbook** database table. The page will display a confirmation and provide a hyperlink to another page where the **guestbook** data can be seen.

guestbook-sign.php

When the page is first loaded the $submit variable will not exist.

```php
<html><head><title>Sign the guestbook</title></head>
<body>
<?php
#the html form
$form = "<form action=\"$PHP_SELF\" method=\"post\">";
$form.= "Name: <input type=\"text\" name=\"name\" ";
$form.= "size=\"50\" value=\"$name\"> <br>";
$form.= "Email: <input type=\"text\" name=\"email\" ";
$form.= "size=\"50\" value=\"$email\"> <br>";
$form.= "Comments:<br>";
$form.= "<textarea name=\"comments\" cols=\"45\" ";
$form.= "rows=\"4\">$comments</textarea> <br>";
$form.= "<input type=\"submit\" name=\"submit\" ";
$form.= "value=\"Sign\"> </form>";

#on first opening display the form
if( !$submit){ $msg = $form; } else

#or redisplay a message and the form if incomplete
if( !$name or !$email or !$comments)
{ $msg = "<b>Please complete all fields</b><br><br>";
  $msg.= $form; } else

#or add the form data to the guestbook database table
{ #connect to MySQL
  $conn = @mysql_connect("localhost", "mike", "bingo")
    or die("Could not connect to database");
```

guestbook-sign.php
(continued)

```php
#select the database
$rs = @mysql_select_db("my_database",$conn)
   or die ("Could not select database");

#create the SQL query
if($name and $comments)
{
   $sql ="insert into guestbook (name, email, comments)
         values (\"$name\",\"$email\",\"$comments\")";
   $rs = @mysql_query($sql,$conn)
         or die ("Could not execute SQL query"); }

#confirm entry and display a link to view guestbook
if($rs)
{ $msg = "<h3>Thank you - your entry has been saved.";
   $msg.= "<br><a href = \"guestbook-view.php\">";
   $msg.= "View My Guestbook</a></h3>"; }
}

#write the page
echo($msg);
?>
</body></html>
```

*This illustration shows the form redisplayed after submission of an incomplete form – there is no entry in the **comments** field. Notice that the previous entries are retained by assigning their PHP variable values to the form's HTML **value** attributes. A successful submission is illustrated on the next page.*

Inserting guestbook entries

*When the form created by the script on the previous page is submitted with entries in all fields the data is added to the **guestbook** database table and a confirmation is displayed.*

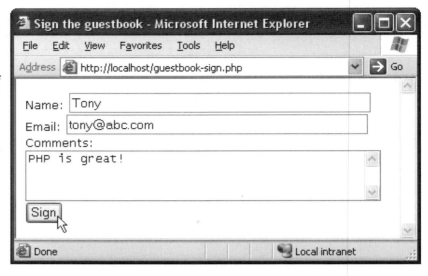

*The record can now be viewed in the MySQL monitor. Notice that data is automatically added to the **id** and **time** fields.*

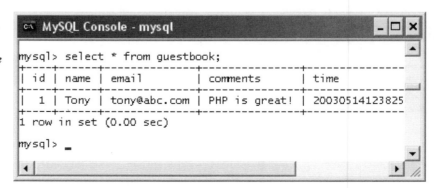

Using timestamp data

The MySQL 14-digit **timestamp** number records the date and time where the first four numbers are the year, then each successive pair of numbers are the month, day number, hour, minutes and seconds.

The PHP **substr()** function can be used to return a part of a timestamp specified as its first argument. Its second argument states the required starting character position as an integer and its third argument specifies the character length of that substring.

timestamp.php

This example splits the **timestamp** shown opposite into separate components. These are made into a time object with the **mktime()** function then formatted for display by the **date()** function— see page 76 for more on date formatting.

```
<html><head><title>Using timestamp</title></head> <body>
<?php $conn=@mysql_connect("localhost", "mike","bingo");
        $rs = @mysql_select_db("my_database",$conn);
        $sql = "select * from guestbook where id=1";
        $rs = @mysql_query($sql,$conn);

#split the timestamp into organized date format
while ($row = mysql_fetch_array( $rs ))
{
  $datetime = $row["time"];
  $year = substr($datetime,0,4);
  $mon  = substr($datetime,4,2);
  $day  = substr($datetime,6,2);
  $hour = substr($datetime,8,2);
  $min  = substr($datetime,10,2);
  $sec  = substr($datetime,12,2);
  $orgdate = date("l F dS, Y h:i A",
              mktime($hour,$min,$sec,$mon,$day,$year));
  echo("Time of entry: ".$orgdate); }
?>
</body></html>
```

The same routine is used in the script on the next page that views entries in the **guestbook** database table.

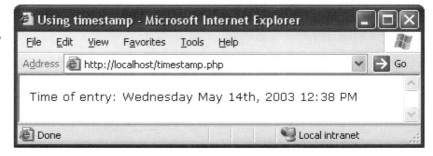

Time of entry: Wednesday May 14th, 2003 12:38 PM

Viewing the guestbook

Following the link on page 182 loads the **guestbook-view.php** script listed below. This extracts the data from each field of the latest three records in the **guestbook** database table, arranged in descending time order.

The script writes a HTML table for each record and displays the stored **name**, **email** address, **comments** and formatted entry **time**.

guestbook-view.php

The SQL query in this example will only extract data from the latest three entries because of the SQL **limit** specifying a value of 3.

```php
<html><head><title>View guestbook</title></head>
<body><h3>Latest 3 guestbook entries...</h3>

<?php
    $rs = @mysql_connect("localhost","mike","bingo");
    $rs = @mysql_select_db("my_database");

    #SQL query for last 3 entries in descending time order
    $sql =
      "select * from guestbook order by time desc limit 3";
    $rs = @mysql_query($sql);

    #loop through records writing a table for each one
    while ($row = mysql_fetch_array($rs))
    {
?>
    <table border="1" width="375">
    <tr>
    <td><b>Name:</b> <? echo $row["name"]; ?></td>
    <td><b>Email:</b>
    <a href="mailto:<? echo $row["email"]; ?>">
    <? echo $row["email"]; ?></a> </td></tr>
    <tr><td colspan="2">

<?php    $datetime = $row["time"];
         $year = substr($datetime,0,4);
         $mon  = substr($datetime,4,2);
         $day  = substr($datetime,6,2);
         $hour = substr($datetime,8,2);
         $min  = substr($datetime,10,2);
         $sec  = substr($datetime,12,2);
         $orgdate = date("l F dS, Y h:i A",
              mktime($hour,$min,$sec,$mon,$day,$year));
?>
```

guestbook-view.php
(continued)

```
Date: <? echo $orgdate; ?></td></tr>
<tr><td colspan="2"><b>Comments:</b>
<? echo $row["comments"]; ?></td></tr>
</table>
<br>

<? } ?>

</body></html>
```

Even with ten entries added to the **guestbook** database table the script only generates HTML tables for each of the last three entries. The visitor's **email** address is formatted as a link with the **mailto:** protocol to make email response simpler.

 Clicking a hyperlink that uses the **mailto:** *protocol will open your default email client application with the target address already completed – just type a reply then send the email response.*

More PHP resources

This book will, hopefully, have provided you with a great introduction to PHP server-side scripting and may have inspired you with some creative possibilities that PHP can achieve.

The many PHP functions used in the examples throughout this book are, in fact, just a small selection from the hundreds of functions that are available in the PHP scripting language. To see the entire range of functions, and to go further with PHP, it is recommended that you now download the PHP manual from **http://www.php.net/download-docs.php**.

The manual is available in several languages and many formats, including HTML, PDF and Windows HLP format. It is very comprehensive and has a section called **Function Reference** that defines each function on its own page. These are grouped under topic headings and many contain examples illustrating how the function can be used in a PHP script.

The **PHP Builder** website at **http://www.phpbuilder.com** is a terrific on-line resource offering interesting articles about PHP. This site also has several forums where help can be sought on PHP scripting. Some source code is available for free download and you can even access the PHP manual on-line here.

Another great on-line resource is the **PHP Resource Index** website at **http://php.resourceindex.com**. This site has lots of useful code snippets and offers hundreds of complete PHP scripts – although not all of these are available free.

The site's **Documentation** section contains examples and tutorials with lots of handy tips. The **Frequently Asked Questions** (FAQ) pages can be scoured for previous answers to PHP questions.

In the **Community** section are links to many PHP-related bulletin boards on the Internet where you can find other PHP developers. There is information about PHP mailing lists, development tools, user groups and lots more.

The huge popularity of PHP as a widely-used scripting language that is especially suited for Web development, ensures its continuing future success – happy scripting with PHP!

Index

! logical not   46
!= inequality operator   50
single-line comment   33
% modulus   44
&& logical and   46
★ multiply   44
+ add   44
++ increment   44
- subtract   44
-- decrement   44
. concatenate strings   44
/ divide   44
/★ ... ★/ multi-line comment   33
// single-line comment   33
< less than operator   50
= assign operator   48
== equality operator   48
=> assign key value   70
> greater than operator   50
? : conditional operator   52
|| logical or   46

array_pop() function   69
array_push() function   68
array_shift() function   69
array_slice() function   72
array_unshift() function   68
as keyword   35, 66
assign data   36
assignment operators   48
attachment form   132
authenticated log-in   176
authorized users   170

backslash character \   34
base64_encode() function   134
boolean data type   37
break keyword   35, 56, 60
browse button   132
browser re-direction   88

access limitation cookie   114
addition   44
advantages of PHP   9
alter table SQL command   147, 163
and keyword   35
and operator   46
Apache
    configuration   16, 24
    installation   12, 22
    starting & stopping   13, 25
appending data   101
array elements   64
array size   67
array() function   64
array_merge() function   72

cache control   86
carriage return \r   130
case keyword   35, 56
case-sensitive   33
chunk_split() function   134
class keyword   35
closedir() function   92
column   140
comments   33
conditional branching   55, 56
continue   35
cookie expiry   111
cookie manager   117
cookies   110
copy file   94
copy() function   94

count() function   67
create database SQL command   156, 158
create table SQL command   143

D

data type specifier   143
database
   records   140
   table columns   140
   table rows   140
   tables   140
date format parameters   76
date() function   76, 182, 184
declare keyword   35
decrement   44
default keyword   35, 56
delete data   149
delete database   157
delete file   96
delete from SQL command   149
delete table   149
desc SQL command   184
die() function   35, 106
directory handle   92
display files   92
display submitted values   81
do keyword   35, 59
do-while loop   59
drop database SQL command   149
drop table SQL command   149

E

echo() function   32, 35
element index number   64
else keyword   35, 55
elseif keyword   35
email address formats   138
email attachments   134

enctype attribute   105, 132
environment variables
   HTTP_REFERER   102, 174
   HTTP_USER_AGENT   74, 90
   PHP_SELF   86, 136
   PHPSESSID   116
   REMOTE_ADDR   102
equality operator   50
error-checking   136
escaping characters   34
eval keyword   35
exit() function   35, 88
explain SQL command   141
extends keyword   35

F

false keyword   35, 37
fclose() function   97, 98
feedback form   127
file input
   _name variable   106
   _size variable   106
   _type variable   106
file input type   105
file modes   97
file pointer   97, 100
file type   105
file_exists() function   100
filesize() function   98
floating-point data type   37
fopen() function   97, 98
for keyword   35
for loop   57
foreach() function   66
form handler   82
form values   80
fread() function   98
function keyword   35, 38
functions   38
   argument   39
   default arguments   42
   multiple   40
   multiple arguments   42
fwrite() function   100